Always Carry Me With You

A young widow's journey of love, loss, and what comes after

Always Carry Me With You

A young widow's journey of love, loss, and what comes after

Faby Ryan

ALEGRIA
PUBLISHING

This book is a memoir and work of creative nonfiction. It reflects the author's recollections of experiences over time and the author's interpretation of conversations that took place. The events are portrayed to the best of the author's memory as some events happened years ago. This book is a combination of fact about a period in the author's life and certain embellishments. While all the stories in this book are true, in order to maintain their anonymity in some instances, some names, and identifying details have been changed to protect the privacy of the people involved. The opinions expressed within this book are the author's personal opinions and are merely freedom of expression.

Library of Congress Control number: 2021923073
ISBN: 9781737992752
Published by Alegria Publishing
Book cover and layout by Carlos Mendoza

For Emma,
The light of my life. The reason and my purpose for everything that I do.

For Danny,
Love of my life. The man who in life and death changed me
in every way a woman can be changed.

Forward

"Your body is away from me,
but there is a window open
from my heart to yours."
- Rumi

Always Carry Me with You pays testament to the transformative powers that live at the heart of our personal stories.

When Faby Ryan embarked on this long-awaited dream of writing her first book,
she had an immense longing to share her story with other women as she dealt with her own grief, hoping that they may feel less alone. Little did she know that this memoir would bring a full catharsis to her own life and her own healing journey.

In the process of writing this memoir and the many writing sessions I participated in as Faby Ryan's mentor, I got to witness her tears co-exist with surprising glimpses of beauty and laughter in the midst of loss, reminding me that duality also welcomes joy.

As her writing mentor, my only real "job" was to make sure Faby felt safe and embraced throughout this process, so that her innate talent as a storyteller could blossom.

And blossom... believe me,

She did.

Both Faby and this book you are now holding have blossomed in the last 12 months, through this artistic process of creation, where both the creator and its reader can sit with their grief and come out at the other side.

What awaits us at the other end of grief and loss?

Does love transcend time and space?

Are we all inherently connected through spirit and unconditional love?

As I read Always Carry Me with You, I can't help but feel Rumi's words come to me:
"Goodbyes are only for those who love with their eyes.
Because for those who love with heart and soul
there is no such thing as separation.
Grief can be the garden of compassion.
If you keep your heart open through everything,
your pain can become your greatest ally in your life's search for love
and wisdom."

Davina A. Ferreira
Founder ALEGRIA Media & Publishing

Contents

Faby Ryan

Preface

Growing up, I never saw myself as the princess who gets rescued at the end of the fairy tale. To me, happily ever after just didn't exist. All the marriages I had ever witnessed had failed, were failing, or were waiting for divorce to happen. As a young girl, I was torn between two worlds: a world of made-up fairy tales (which I really wanted to believe existed), and a world where nothing ever worked out. While marrying Prince Charming and the idea of happily ever after was most of my friends' dreams, that just wasn't a thing for my future. I had other plans for myself, plans that included one day becoming a writer and sharing my stories with the world. The ideas of building a life with someone and marriage were terrifying to me. The thought of children was even more terrifying. I never saw myself as motherly. I had endured too much pain and trauma as a child that had made me never want to bring children of my own into the world.

As life would have it with its twists and turns, any and all ideas of Prince Charming I ever had would completely change when my knight in shining crutches walked into my life and forever changed my story. Yes, you read that right. There was no white horse or shining armor; there were crutches and dirt bikes and boats, oh my! I met Danny at a point in my life when I was incredibly focused on my studies and myself, and still trying to get over a broken heart. I was not in a good place to date, never mind be in a relationship, but Danny was persistent, a go getter—unlike any other man I had ever met. He was genuine, kind, loving, and incredibly funny—a man with the most beautiful smile.

At twenty-five, and after only nine months of dating, I married this man, the love of my life. And becoming a mother soon became the one thing I desired most. It turned out the story I thought I never wanted had been everything I needed, and one that would change my life forever. Marrying Danny changed me in every way a person can be changed. But as fate would have it, our story was like no other, and it took us on a journey unlike any I ever imagined. It was a journey of love, hope, resilience, healing, and purpose. And, yes, lots of hardship, grief, and pain, too. But given the choice, I would endure it all over again if it meant sharing my life with such an incredible man and becoming a mother to the most amazing little miracle created by our love. I know I wouldn't be the person I am today had it not been for the life I've lived, the experiences that have shaped me, and the journey of love, hope, loss, resilience, and what comes after. It's not the typical fairy tale with its happily ever after ending, but this is my unique story.

As I sit here today, about to share my story with the world, I can't help but think about choices. If I'd never allowed love into my life, if I'd shut myself off from the ideas of love, marriage, and children because of my fears as a young girl, I would never have known what true love and happiness is. While my love story doesn't end the way I wished it had, I'm glad the choices I made led to me meeting and loving one of the best persons I've ever come to know—not perfect by any means, but perfect for me. We are all one choice away from the rest of our lives, and this was mine. Though I wish some parts of my story had never happened, they have inspired me to live a life with purpose, to appreciate more, and to find my joy. I hope with my words and through my story I can inspire you, too. That on the days you feel you can't go on, you might just realize you can. And you will.

If you would have told me that at thirty-eight years old, in the middle of a global pandemic, and in the midst of grief I would be writing and publishing a memoir, I would never have believed it. But here I am, terrified of the unknown and ready for anything life throws my way.

This book is for anyone who has ever loved. Anyone who has experienced loss or grief. And anyone who has embarked on the journey to finding what comes after.

Faby Ryan

I Love You

I'm scared to love you, because I'm scared to lose you.

The first time I said, "I love you," I hadn't expected to say it. In fact, I hadn't really thought of it. Those three little words that get used way too often and so loosely meant too much to me to just say them to anyone. And although Danny had become someone incredibly special to me, the thought of saying "I love you" was scary to me. Throughout our relationship, Danny made it a point of reminding me how much he really, really liked me and how incredibly afraid he was I would break his heart; ironic, because that had always been my biggest fear in any and all relationships. "Tell me if you don't like me, because I really like you. And if you don't, that's gonna suck, but I rather hear it from you now than later, so if you don't like me just tell me," he'd say often.

"Slow it down," I would tell him. "The faster you take it, the sooner it ends. Let's just take things slow." Slow was good. I needed slow. I mean, it had taken me five weeks just to call him after he gave me his number, but Danny had waited long enough; he was not about to take anything slow. He got excited easily and got antsy altogether. Patience was not his forte, especially when it came to our relationship. When Danny set his heart on me, he went all in. He never held back or played games like I'd been used to from guys in previous relationships. He was eager to "win me over" but in the most genuine, kind, and loving of ways. I remember on our first unofficial date (the day before our official set date, because he couldn't wait another day to see me) he took me to Palos Verdes on a hike along the cliffs overlooking the ocean. "To pregame," he said. I later learned "pregame" was a thing he liked to do a lot.

That mid-May Saturday morning, we walked along the hills in the salty ocean air in Palos Verdes, CA, the perfectly warm spring sun shining the way through the trails. We talked for hours about everything and nothing. Danny was so easy to talk to and had a way of making me laugh like no other. He never took himself too seriously, which was kind of refreshing. By mid-afternoon that day, I felt like I'd known him longer than I had. We ended our hike on this little bench that would become *our bench,* a place he decided matter-of-factly we would for sure come back to. After our hike, we went back to his place in Torrance, about a thirty-minute drive from where we were. Honestly, I'm not sure why I agreed to this. I barely knew this guy, and now I was going back to his place; who was I? I think I was still on a high and filled with happy endorphins from our incredible hike. *How did he know this was the way to my heart?* Once we were at his place, Danny decided he wanted to cook for me, BBQ to be exact, except he had nothing ready and nothing in his pantry. So, this guy decided to leave me at his place to go grocery shopping. I think he was just trying to impress me by showing off his independence and kitchen skills, which totally worked. "I'll come with you," I insisted, but he wanted to do it all by himself, all for me.

"You're my guest; let me take care of you." And so, he did. Next thing I knew he was grilling up burgers, veggies, and BBQ beans. *I could get used to this*, I thought. *Who doesn't love a man who can cook?!* After dinner, he took me into his garage to show me his pride and joy project: a race boat engine he'd been building for years.

"Did you really do this all yourself?" I asked. It was incredible. His face glowed when he spoke of this project. I knew nothing about boats, engines, or machinery, but it was beautiful to see. Needless to say, we had an amazing "pregame" date. It was easy—no pressure at all. He got to see me just how I was, and I, him. No masks or appearances put up.

The following day for our "official" first date, I was actually a bit nervous, surprisingly. I wanted Danny to see me outside of my work uniforms and hiking attire. I wanted him to see me dressed up, in heels and a dress—a hottie. I wanted to impress him and rock his world. Plus, any excuse to dress up was always a win for me. I knew we were going to dinner in Hermosa Beach, but Danny wouldn't tell me more. I wanted to play it safe, so I wore a silky, fitted, off-the-shoulder long sleeve little black dress that fell right above the knees. The long sleeves were chiffon and patterned with a beautiful magenta accent detail. I had the perfect closed-toe pointed heels to match. I straightened my hair for the occasion, which I often do when I go out. My makeup was a semi-smokey eye, perfect for an evening look, paired with the perfect nude lip.

I was anxious and excited. I hadn't dated in a while, so those first date butterflies were really fluttering. I couldn't wait to see Danny. I was curious to know what his "going out" looked like, too. Little did I know Danny was not the dressing up type; he was simple. He could live in flip flops and shorts all day every day, but for me, he dressed up. He wore jeans, a button up shirt, skater shoes, and a black jacket (which would become his favorite). He looked cute. As a true gentleman, he came up to the door, which I hesitated to open (*such a girl!*). He walked me to the car, opened the door for me, and out we went.

"Where are we going?" I asked.

"It's a surprise."

We drove down to Hermosa Beach to a cute little Italian restaurant near The Strand. We had an amazing dinner paired with yummy red wine. Later, I learned Danny wasn't a wine guy; I for sure wasn't going to have that. I turned him into a wine guy in no time! We talked endlessly at dinner; I mean, you couldn't get us to shut up even if you tried. After dinner, we walked over to the comedy and magic club for the evening show, where Jay Leno was headlining. Dinner, wine, and a good laugh—this was my kind of date!

Inside the comedy club, we sat in the dark at a little cocktail table toward the back (it was all they had, don't get any ideas) and ordered drinks. We couldn't stop laughing and talking. We seemed to be more interested in our conversation than the comedians, so much so, that we got shushed one too many times and almost got kicked out of the place. Hey, what can I say? We had lots to say! We ended that night at a little 80s café down the road, drinking milkshakes until 1 am. We had a wonderful time, and I knew this guy was going to stir up my life. We ended the night with the most wonderful first kiss. The kind of kiss I hoped for: long and gentle, with the perfect intensity. Danny, I learned that night, was an amazing kisser.

As much as I'd hesitated at first, Danny and I became inseparable. He had this way of making me feel special and important in his life. Even when he was out of town or on the road for work, which was often at the time. He always made sure I knew he was thinking of me. He'd send me flowers to work just because. He'd stop by before and after every trip to say good morning or good night. We would spend hours on end on the phone, and if we were not together, we'd be chatting in a chat room online or over email. "I'm falling asleep," he'd say. "We can't keep staying up this late; you hang up." It was beautiful back then—no social media like there is today. Things were more intimate and personal. Or maybe I am just old school. I love old school.

Soon, Danny introduced me to his family—his entire family—on the Fourth of July. Every year on this day, his family would get together at Grandma Vi's, his great grandmother's, to celebrate. "You have to come this year," he said. "There is no way you can't come. I want you to meet my Grams and the rest of the family."

So, I did. All at once, I met parents, stepparents, brother, stepsiblings, cousins, aunts and uncles, friends of the family, and lots and lots of nieces and nephews. It was a full house and super intimidating to say the least. I was used to big families—I have one myself, but I never expected his to be this big. We ended up having a great time. We rode bikes around the neighborhood to and from my house. Grandma Vi's house was literally three minutes from the house my parents lived in, and I knew that neighborhood pretty well. My friend and ex-co-worker, Brittany, lived in the area, too, so we ended up crashing her block party for part of the day.

Danny's family was welcoming, especially his dad, and I soon realized the amazing bond they had with one another. I also met and immediately fell in love with Grandma Vi. She was the sweetest lady with the kindest, most beautiful blue eyes. She transmitted love, pure love. I felt welcomed by her instantly. I always did. She passed years later. The night before she passed, I talked to her and held her hand until she fell asleep. She was in and out of consciousness, but she always knew who I was. I felt her love, and I know she felt mine. Fourth of July at Grams's will always have a special place in my heart.

On Danny's 29th birthday, I decided to plan a special date for him. He had been so incredible to me that I wanted to do something for him. Up until this point, he had been the one to let me know how he felt about me, while I was still incredibly hesitant. But on this day, I asked him out officially, or so he says I did. We never quite worked that part out. I took him to dinner at Moon Shadows in Malibu to celebrate, and after dessert I asked, "So, do you wanna make this official?!" He laughed and giddily said yes! That was the beginning of a beautiful relationship. The beginning of Faby and Danny.

Danny was a lover. He had so much love in his heart to give, and with me, he never held back. Soon after we made it official, Danny said "I love you" for the first time. It scared the bejesus out of me. I really liked him, and I felt his sincerity, but I couldn't say it back. I wasn't ready. I told him I really liked him, and I loved spending time with him, but I didn't want to say I love you just because he'd said it. I wanted to be absolutely sure when I did say it. He was bummed, but he understood, and I think he respected me a little bit more for being true to myself and being honest. I just needed a little time.

One night after work, Danny and I went to a local restaurant/ bar hangout spot to grab a bite to eat, and it just so happened to be karaoke night. I love me a good karaoke night! Of course, Danny encouraged me to sign up to sing, so I did. I was suddenly so nervous when they called my name to get up there and sing. *What was I thinking?* My heart started to race so fast and so loud, I was afraid the mic would pick up on it. Danny took a front row seat and stared at me intently as the music started to play. *Holy shit what am I doing?!* And then the song "But I Do Love You" by LeAnn Rimes started.

I stared into Danny's eyes the entire song. He stared right back at mine. For a moment there, the entire room disappeared, and it was just us two. I felt every word and spoke each lyric straight from my heart to his. It suddenly hit me: I loved this man. I was in love with this man. It was a miracle I finished he song. I was full of emotion and as much as I wanted the song to end, I also didn't. I wanted this moment to last. As I walked back to my seat, cheering and chatter around me, I kept my eyes on Danny. Standing in front of him, I said it, as though the song hadn't already been clear enough.

"I love you."

He held and kissed me, then whispered, "I know."

Super Date

When I met you
I didn't know this type of love existed
Now I know what it truly means to feel loved.

The night Danny proposed, I thought I saw it coming, but I had it all wrong. We had been dating for nine months at this point. "I love yous" had been exchanged. We'd met each other's families. My family loved him. And I thought his liked me, too. We spent every opportunity we could with each other. We couldn't stay away. We were in love. Everyone could see it. It floated in the air.

One Friday night in early December, Danny said to me, "Babe, on Sunday, I'm gonna take you on a super date!"

"A super date?" I replied, "But you haven't lost a bet?!"

"I want to do it for you! I love you; just go with it."

Now, let me explain to you what a super date is and why it became such an important part of our life and our marriage and a way to fill our love cup. It all started with a simple "How much you wanna bet?" And because we didn't know what to bet, I said, "I bet you a date."

Danny, being Danny, had to up the ante and said, "I bet you a super date!"

"A super date?" I asked.

"Yes," Danny said, "whoever loses the bet has to take the other on an over-the-top date. He/she has to plan every single detail. And, it must be a surprise!"

He had me at surprise. "It's a bet!"

Danny lost the first one. I'm not even sure what the bet was, really, but the super date I clearly remember. Danny planned this night for two weeks. He was so cute trying to be extra sneaky. It took everything for him not to spill the beans, but all he could tell me was when to be ready. It was mid-fall, a little chilly, and I didn't know what we were doing so I played it safe and wore a tangerine maxi dress. It was still sexy but covered enough just in case it got cold. Danny picked me up in my bedroom, dressed in my favorite washed denim Hudson Jeans, which made his butt look really good; a brown button up shirt; and black dress shoes. He looked so handsome, and I was beyond excited.

First, Danny took me to dinner in Newport Beach at one of those Japanese teppanyaki places we'd grown to love. We had a few laughs as the chef did his tricks on the grill and made us catch some shrimp he tossed across the table into our mouths. We enjoyed a glass of wine as we ate our dinner, which was delicious. Dinner was followed by a gondola cruise in the Newport Beach canals. It was so cute! I didn't know this at the time, but Danny even went to HomeGoods, one of my favorite stores, and handpicked and bought a wicker basket for the occasion.

Once at the gondola spot, he showed up with the wicker basket filled with two wine bottles, light snacks, napkins, and a cozy blanket for the evening cruise, all which he'd been hiding in the back seat of the truck the entire time. I was impressed with his attention to detail and all the love he put into the evening surprise. Danny definitely knew my love language. This was the best super date! The gondola ride was incredibly romantic. We cruised the canals right before sunset and we toasted our glasses, "To us!" The guy paddling the boat singing in Italian the entire time was the cherry on top; we got a kick out of that. That evening, we had one of the most romantic and exhilarating date nights. The anticipation and the not knowing, but knowing something great was coming, made it all the more fun. We were on to something here. And thank God I had won this bet. I planned on winning them all moving forward. Danny had set the bar high.

Super dates couldn't just be thrown lightly, we'd decided; they could only be used when it meant business. The time and effort that went into putting them together was a lot, Danny had discovered. And of course, the game was on. We both tried so hard to win, but I lost the next super date bet, and the pressure was on. Although Danny was mostly easygoing and simple, he was not the easiest to impress. I had to think of something manly and dude-ish to do, not an easy task for this girly girl. But I loved a challenge and was determined. I was a hopeless romantic. *This is gonna be a piece of cake,* I thought. Boy, was it not that easy.

You know that whole women are from Venus, men are from Mars thing? So me! What could I possibly do for Danny that was not all gooey and romantic? I had come up with the best idea, or at least I thought it was. I took him on a beachfront sunset picnic, which I had my sister help me set up prior to the date. I don't know that Danny enjoyed the romantic white linen and red roses at sunset as much as I did, but hey, it was my first take! At dinner, I handed him (almost) courtside Lakers tickets. The game was phenomenal. Danny had never been to a Lakers game, and they won of course: win–win. And although I lost a bet, I had an incredible time putting the day together for Danny. We had an amazing date with a happy ending. Always a happy ending!

If I remember correctly, Danny lost more bets than I did throughout our life together, but I think he secretly enjoyed it. These anticipatory dates became a fun part of our story. A way to add an extra something to our relationship. Neither of us really cared about who won or lost the bets. We both just enjoyed putting them together for each other. They were an opportunity to have fun, to bond, to go the extra mile and to love a little extra, expecting nothing in return. Super dates became a big part of our love story.

So, on this particular Friday evening in December, Danny had caught me by surprise telling me he wanted to take me on a super date when he hadn't lost a bet. I, of course agreed to the date, but I was also left wondering what he was up to. I had a funny feeling Danny was planning something bigger than a super date, and I mentioned to my sister, "I think Danny's proposing!"

"Why do you think that?" my sister asked.

"I don't know. I just have a feeling."

"I doubt it," she said. "I think you're imagining things." And that was that.

Sunday morning, as I was getting ready for my impromptu super date, my mom walked into my room and said, "You know, I really like Danny. He's such a great guy, and I can tell he loves you very much!"

"Why are you telling me this?" I asked.

"No reason. I just really like Danny." *There is definitely something fishy going on here. What if he does propose?*

"I think Danny's going to propose," I told her.

"Why do you think that? I don't think so," she replied before walking out of my room.

Danny picked me up around five for our super date. He looked extra handsome with his favorite long-sleeved brown pinstriped dress shirt and denim jeans. Dressy casual, as I called it. He hopped on the Long Beach freeway and headed toward Alamitos Bay at the Long Beach marina. I kept looking at him inquisitively the entire time, wondering what he was up to until we came to a stop. We pulled up to The Crab Pot for dinner. *The Crab Pot? But I'm wearing a white dress!* was all I was thinking. The Crab Pot is a seafood place where they dump the food right on your table and they give you a plastic bib so you can go to town. *Casual dinner—he definitely isn't proposing. But what if he does?*

We had a lovely meal. We laughed, we toasted with a yummy red bottle of wine, the bill came, and nothing. No proposal. *Maybe I am imagining things.* After dinner, Danny asked me if I wanted to walk around and go see the boats. In December, Long Beach has a really cool boat parade where they decorate the boats with beautiful Christmas lights, play music, and go all out in Christmas décor. "Sure," I said, and to the boat parade we went.

Maybe he'll propose at the lights? We watched the sun go down as we walked the bay. Pink, purple, and orange hues filled the sky. It was beautiful and so peaceful. Danny and I talked about how happy we were in our relationship thus far, how much we got along, and how much we had in common even though we came from different worlds, he being white and I, Hispanic. I had never met someone that understood me and accepted me—the real me flaws and all—the way Danny did. I was incredibly happy.

The night turned dark, and Danny suggested we get going. *Seriously? He's not proposing?!* We started to head to the car when Danny asked if I wanted to go to candy cane lane and walk around and maybe get some hot cocoa. *Maybe he wants to propose at candy cane lane.* Candy cane lane is a super popular area in Torrance, CA, where blocks and blocks of houses decorate for Christmas. People from all over come every year and either drive or walk around for hours to see it all. It's quite the destination. "The night is still young," I said, "let's go!"

Once at candy cane lane, we grabbed some hot cocoa, which some of the locals sell to visitors, and walked around looking at some of our favorite homes, which displayed life-size nativity scenes, projector screens, and even a carrousel. Danny held me close and tried to keep me warm from the cool evening air. *I love you, Daniel John.* Our love for each other was as evident as the lights that covered the streets. *Is he going to propose here?* Danny and I walked and walked holding hands until we tired out. "You ready to go?" Danny asked.

"I think so," I said, and we headed out. No proposal.

On our drive home, Danny started to not feel so well. "I need to stop," he said, "Maybe it was the hot cocoa, but I don't think I can make it home." He pulled over at a Starbucks and ran in without even shutting off the car. "Stay in the car," he yelled as he ran out.

When he was done, he jumped back in the car and we got going again. "Are you ok?" I kept asking.

"I think we should call it a night," he said. I'd had a wonderful night, but I was a little bummed. First, this whole proposal thing had been in my head, and now Danny wasn't feeling well. Usually, after every date, we'd go back to Danny's place to hang out for a while and unwind for the night. I wasn't sure this would be the case this time, but then he asked, "Do you want me to take you home, or do you want to hang out at my place for just for a little?"

"Let's hang out, even for a little." I was so bummed, but I wanted ed to make sure Danny was ok too. We pulled into his driveway, and Danny handed me the keys and asked if I could open the door. I grabbed the keys and went ahead. When I walked in, I couldn't believe my eyes. The room was filled with candles and roses everywhere. I stood there in shock. *What is happening? Is this real?* When I looked back at Danny, he was right behind me, down on one knee, holding a ring in his hands.

I can't tell you how he started his speech, or what he said, but once I came to, all I heard was, "Faby, I love you and I want to spend the rest of my life with you. Will you marry me?!"

Tears were flowing down my face. *Is this really happening?!* I'd been imagining this happening the entire day, but at this point I had already put it out of my brain. I was genuinely not expecting it. I kneeled down to kiss him, and with tears still streaming, I said, "YES!

Of course, I will marry you!"

Emotions were flowing incredibly high. I was in disbelief. I was filled with love. Joy. Confusion. He picked me up and held me for what felt like forever. Danny was so nervous; I could feel his body still shaking. He grabbed my left hand and placed a beautiful white gold, princess cut diamond on my ring finger.

"Are we really doing this?! We're getting married?"

"Yes, we are, future Mrs. Ryan!"

We toasted with a glass a champagne to celebrate, then Danny carried me into the bedroom where we made love the entire night.

★★★

I didn't know this at the time, but both my mom and sister were in on the proposal. Earlier that week, Danny called my mom and asked if he could come over and talk to her and my dad. "What does he want to talk about?" my dad asked. "You know I don't like talking; my English is terrible!" My dad is extremely self-conscious about his English, just as much as Danny was about his attempts at Spanish, but between hand gestures and broken languages, they always made it work.

Friday night while I was at work, Danny went over to my parents' and with all the nerves in the world, he sat and asked them for my hand in marriage. "I want to marry your daughter; I love her," Danny explained. "Momma, what do you say?" Danny asked my mom. My mom was in tears as soon as she realized what was happening. She loved Danny very much and knew how much I loved him. Danny won my mom over from day one. She loved his personality, sense of humor, and how he was always himself. Danny was comfortable in any situation, even when he was out of his element. He was already a son to her.

"You have my blessing," she told him.

"And you, Chato?" Chato is what everyone calls my dad.

"Whatever she said," was his nervous reply, and they all laughed and celebrated what I didn't know was coming.

That Sunday morning, it was no wonder why both my mom and sister were acting weird. They knew what was about to happen and wanted to assure me they loved Danny, but in doing so, they almost gave his surprise away. I have great instincts and intuition. It's hard to get anything past me. When Danny realized I was on to him, he changed his initial plan of proposing at the Christmas lights and made up that whole charade of being sick to trick me. He quickly called my sister and asked her to help him set up his house with the flowers and candles for the grand finale. My sister was Danny's go-to and she was always game for all of his craziness. I loved the relationship between them.

The relationship between my siblings and our significant others was always very important to us. I wanted them to meet Danny before we got serious, just like I had met their significant others. The bond between them and us had to be strong if we wanted a good family dynamic. Danny felt the same way. Before introducing Danny to my family, Danny turned to me and said, "If your family doesn't like me, break up with me!" I look at him baffled.

"What?!" I replied.

"You heard me right; family is important and if they don't like me, this will not work." He was right. When you build a relationship with someone, it goes beyond the two people in love. Family is important, especially in our case where we both came from different backgrounds and cultures. It was important to us that our families approved.

When I heard the backstory of the days leading up to my proposal, it made me love Danny even more. Danny was caring and respectful to my parents—enough to talk to them before proposing to me. This was the most important question of my life. One that would change everything. Danny including my family in such a huge decision meant the world to me. It had always been very important to Danny that my family liked and accepted him. My family not only liked him, but they also loved him.

Danny was easy to love. He was helpful and caring to those around him. It didn't matter who it was. He always made an effort to include everyone and make them feel at home. He learned to communicate through hand signals and broken Spanish with my family members who didn't speak English—particularly my Mami Celia who didn't speak a word of English. "*Hola* grandma," he would say. "*Una cerveza?*" A beer? I would find him laughing and chatting away with her in his humorous broken Spanish. She just laughed with him. They had a special bond. When I lost my Mami Celia in early 2015 to cancer, Danny stood by me every step of the way. We had both lost our grandmas.

I always admired Danny's charisma and ability to embrace people. I knew bringing Danny into the family was the right decision, not only for me and my future but for my family as well. They gained a son and brother. Danny came into our world to change and spice it up a little. With his laughter, joy, and love for life, he taught me and my family a lot about how to live life to the fullest.

DJR

Daniel John Ryan, the boy who stole my heart,
the boy with the three first names.

When I met Danny, I wasn't really sure if we'd hit it off. We were from very different worlds. Danny was an Irish-Italian boy, full of life and spunk who loved to go camping, dirt bike riding, boating, and all the sporty, outdoorsy things I knew nothing about. And I was the wildly curly-haired, spicy Latina and social butterfly, as he called me, who loved working with people, music, and anything in the arts. I wasn't Danny's usual type, but I was just what he'd been looking for. Danny, although not my usual type either, was unlike anyone I'd ever met. Once I got to know him, he quickly had my attention. Unlike anyone I had ever dated, he was a lot more interesting. The more I learned, the more I wanted to know about him.

At the very young age of fifteen, Danny had already expressed a love for working with his hands; machining was something he loved to do. By the time he was sixteen, he was already a manual machinist at a company in El Segundo, CA. Soon after that, he taught himself how to code and operate a mill. By 1999, at twenty years old, Danny worked at Cosworth Racing as a manufacturing engineer with the big boys. He was involved in the stages of manufacturing, design, programming, and machining. After Cosworth, at twenty-six, he moved on to Honda racing as a research and development engineer and superbike engine builder. Let me add, most of this was self-taught. Danny had taken some courses in college in Blueprint, CAD CAM, SolidWorks, Mastercam, and Unigraphics, but most of his experience was gained by doing the work. Danny wasn't the book-smart type, he had always been very hands-on and street-smart, a natural.

I met Danny when he was twenty-eight, when he was still at Honda Racing. I clearly remember on one of our first "meet ups," he took me to his work, showed me around the shop, and was so excited and proud to show me what he'd been building. Danny took so much pride in his work. On the side, he was building a race boat/race boat engine. On our first unofficial date when he took me into his garage to see it, he gleamed with pride. He could have talked endlessly of his plan, his execution, and his future with that boat, but for the sake of our date, he stopped himself. This was only one of his side projects; additionally, he had dirt bikes and everything that had to do with racing and fixing and building. This guy blew me away. Not only was he absolutely charming and kind and funny, he was damn smart.

I was excited to hear Danny's stories and see his craft, but honestly, this was a whole new world to me. I knew nothing of engines and dirt bikes—Supercross who?! Dating Danny was an adventure in itself. He broadened my world and showed me things I never knew existed.

In 2008, a few months after we started dating, Danny got the opportunity of a lifetime as a structures engineer for an up-and-coming company named SpaceX, or Space Exploration Technologies. I remember us sitting on his living room floor at the rental house he lived in, in Torrance, CA, and him showing me the email. Danny was hesitant to take the job. He wasn't sure he had the skills for aerospace. Danny was never a show-off; on the contrary, he used to downplay his capabilities. I could see miles away how capable and smart he was, but Danny was just very humble, a quality I loved and admired. After talking it through, he decided to go for it. In June 2008, he had his first interview at SpaceX. In July he had a second interview, which included interviewing with Chris Hansen and Elon Musk. By the end of July, he had a job offer, and on August 25, 2008, he showed up for his first day of work. Although intimidated and doubtful when he first started at the company, Danny went on to have an amazing seven-year career at SpaceX, where he grew so much as an engineer and within the company. While SpaceX was not an easy job and required a lot of my husband, it was a great place that always took care of him and us. We made amazing friends that we continued to keep in contact with and who later became an immense support system to Emma and me. I will forever be grateful to this company and the opportunities it gave our family.

So how did this outdoorsy Irish-Italian and sassy Latina hit it off? We were both larger than life. We were both fun and loud and spunky and happy. We could also be stubborn and set in our ways, but we always found a way to be a team and work together on the things that were important, not just on the fun stuff that anyone could do. Danny and I saw each other with love and pride. I was so proud of my husband, and I know he was immensely proud of me. And more than that, we both had incredible work ethic and made similar decisions, even before meeting each other. When Danny and I met, we asked the hard questions, not just the surface stuff people tend to ask each other. We both literally had our own lists that we needed to check off in order to make this relationship work, and it is probably not the list you are thinking of.

"Do you smoke? Because if you do, that's a deal breaker."

"No? No, ok!"

"Do you have any debt? 'Cause I have none, and I can't deal with irresponsibility."

"No? No, ok!"

"What do you think about relationships being 50/50?"

"I think they should be 100/100."

"Same, score!"

"Have you ever been married?"

"Engaged."

"Same, ok!"

And the list went on. What is your relationship with your parents like? What do you think about children and religion? What is on your list for the next five years?

It turned out Danny and I had more in common than I'd ever had with anyone before. We were blown away. There weren't a lot of similarities in our lifestyles, but at our core, we were a perfect match.

As the years went on, Danny taught me everything there was to know about camping, the desert, dirt bikes, boating, and the list goes on. I tried it all. I jumped on a dirt bike and fell on my ass a few times. I learned how to drive a boat and tow him as he skied. I perfected pulling the boat from the water onto the trailer in one shot—Danny was very impressed. I camped and got dirty, even when all his friends, especially the women, made fun of me. I didn't care. I laughed it off and carried on. I even learned about mills and lathes because he lived in the garage tinkering with his tools. More often than not I'd bring a bottle of wine into the garage, and we would sip as he worked and smelled of tool grease.

I taught Danny everything there was to know about music and art and fashion. I loved working and helping people, something which he later joined me in. Years later, Danny confessed he'd fallen in love with me very early on; he knew I was the one after seeing me use sign language with a customer. *It is your giving heart, my love,* he would always say. I played the guitar and the piano and once or twice tried to get him to pick up a tune. Instead, he bought me a better guitar because he said mine sucked. Man, how I love that guitar! I shared with him my poetry, my writing, and my love for books. I promised him that one day, I would write a book. Danny was not a reader; I don't think he ever finished a book in his life, but once in a while, for me, he tried. As different as Danny and I were, we were also very alike. Above all, we had immense respect for each other. Danny pushed me to better every day; he encouraged me to follow my dreams. *Whatever you want to do, babe, I support you,* I can still hear him say. And I always supported him and his dreams, too.

I do

Just us, for us, promising forever.

Danny and I celebrated our engagement by throwing ourselves a party a couple weeks after getting engaged. It was an intimate party at Danny's place with our closest friends and family. We cleaned and set up the backyard with round tables with burgundy overlays (to make it a little fancy) and hung twinkling lights everywhere for an added touch. We didn't want to cater the party as we were trying to save for our wedding, so Danny decided to prepare an Italian feast: his famous Italian spaghetti sauce. We had music, lit a bonfire, played games, and danced, laughed, and toasted the night away as everyone celebrated our future. It was perfect.

Little did anyone know that on January 9, 2009, only a month and two days after our engagement, Danny and I were getting married in secret. Between our engagement and January 9th, Danny and I threw ourselves an engagement party, moved in together, got our marriage license, shopped for our wedding bands, and made an appointment at the LAX courthouse to be married. It was a Friday, the only day they performed marriages, and we had to be at the courthouse by 8:30 am to be married at 9 am. We got up extra early and anxious for the day's event.

"Good morning soon to be Mrs. Ryan," Danny said when he woke up.

"I can't believe we are doing this!" we said in excitement.

We drove to the courthouse, dressed for the casual event. I wore blue jeans and a white heart-shaped chiffon halter top; I figured something white would be nice. And Danny wore blue jeans, a red t-shirt (his favorite color), and a black dressy jacket. It was perfect— just us, as us, nothing fancy. We arrived at the courthouse and were met by my mom and sister. We had to tell them as we needed two witnesses, and I just had to have them there with me.

At exactly 9 am, the judge called our name. My heart was pounding, and tears started welling up in my eyes. The room we were being married in had an arch set up that was decorated with artificial flowers. Under said arch we would say our I dos. The judge was already waiting at the end of a tiny aisle. I didn't expect to get as emotional as I did, but the intimacy of our marriage and the fact that it was only for us made it even more special than I realized. As Danny and I stood before the judge saying our vows, promising forever, and exchanging rings, I fell in love with him even more. We looked into each other's eyes filled with tears and sealed the moment with the perfect kiss. I was so glad my mom and sister had been there to witness and be a part of our special day. I think they were crying, too. The room was filled with the perfect amount of people and an abundance of love.

After our marriage ceremony, Danny and I took a moment to ourselves and kissed goodbye. He had to get back to work as he hadn't been able to take the day off due to his responsibilities. I still laugh at that fact today: we married and parted ways, ha! After we left the courthouse, I took my sister and mom out for breakfast at our favorite Denny's in our old neighborhood in Hawthorne, CA, where we cheered with coffee to Danny and me. Again, nothing fancy. But the day was perfect.

Disney World

I never believed in fairy tales, until I met you.

"I'm so excited for Disney World, Mommy, I can't believe we are actually going on a plane. I can't wait to meet Elsa and Anna. Do you think I can get a picture with them? I can't wait to get there, Mommy. How long is the ride? When will we get there? Thank you for my birthday present, Mommy. Are you excited?!" Emma talked excitedly as she took the window seat and looked out at the flag on the wing of the plane. It was 8:30 am. 2016. A beautiful mid-May day with clear skies. The view looked like it was going to be an amazing one.

"Of course, I'm excited too, peanut. Of course I'm excited, too!" I replied.

As a child, I always loved Disneyland—the characters, the rides, the music, the princesses. I always dreamt of being cast as a Disney princess: Princess Jasmine, from *Aladdin*; I thought she was perfect. Or maybe Princess Belle from *Beauty and the Beast*. They looked more like me than any of the other princesses: caramel skin, dark hair, and beautiful brown eyes; plus, I knew every song and line from the movies. *What a dream job that would be*, the little dreamer girl in me always thought.

Living in Southern California, Hawthorne, to be exact, getting to Disneyland was pretty convenient. Anaheim, where the park was located, was only thirty minutes away. We didn't go to Disneyland as often as we would have liked because for a family of five, Disneyland got pretty expensive. My parents worked extremely hard—my mom was a cosmetologist and my dad worked in construction—but times were always hard. We didn't have much money to spare, but my mom was an incredible budgeter. Once in a while, she'd budget just enough with some to spare, and she would surprise us with a treat somewhere. A few of these times, the treat was a trip to Disneyland, the happiest place on earth, and happy we sure were. I remember the first time I met Minnie and Mickey at their house; talk about magical dreams coming true. I still hold on to my old Disneyland signature book with their autographs in it, a little treasure that I have passed on to Emma.

As I took my seat on the plane next to Emma, who was filled with every emotion and excitement, my mind traveled back to the summer of 2008. It was a beautiful, hot, mid-June day. Danny and I had just started "hanging out." We weren't officially dating yet, because I was terrified at the ideas of dating and a relationship, but here was this really nice guy who really liked me and I'd agreed to hang out and be friends. This particular mid-June summer day, June 18th to be exact, I took him on a date to Disneyland. I was very excited to go so I planned the entire thing. Now, no guy ever says, "Sure baby, let's go on a date to Disneyland!" unless your guy's idea of a romantic date is to walk around all day, stand in long lines with a bunch of screaming kids, ride on teacups, and take pictures with a bunch of grown-ups in stuffed costumes. But it was my idea, and since he really liked me and knew how much I wanted to go, he happily accepted.

I have always been a happy-go-lucky kid at heart, so if you take me to Disneyland, I am like a kid again. This time I was especially excited. I never told Danny, but secretly I was hoping for this hang out to turn into a real date, something a little more than just "hanging out." After a bad previous break-up, I was scared to let anyone into my world, my heart, my personal space. Maybe this place would be where we could let loose and not put so much pressure on things—not that we didn't already act like kids at times, but here we could definitely be silly and get in touch with our inner kids again. It was perfect—my happy place. I had never brought a date with me to Disneyland before, so it was kind of a big deal to me. Spending an entire day together, that could either be a great thing, or a complete disaster.

The date started off a little rocky, though. I planned to meet a friend and her boyfriend there for a double date, thinking it would be more fun. I didn't know if the guys just didn't hit it off or what, but it got awkward and tense for a minute. Danny wasn't himself (the super fun and outgoing guy I had come to know), he was quiet and seemed annoyed. I was thrown off and thought, *Maybe this was a mistake,* but the last thing I wanted to do was hurt my friend's feelings and end the date. I had been looking forward to this so much. Disneyland brought me happy memories of my childhood. Just entering the Disneyland Park for me was a whole new world, no pun intended. I have always been amazed with the attention to detail: The art. The lights. The colors. The love stories. Yes, I am a hopeless romantic. And I wanted to experience this with Danny. The idea of this date not working out was breaking my fairy-tale-loving little heart. We almost ended the date, but later in the day, our friends ended up going home early.

It was like magic, the happy-go-lucky, fun, funny, attentive Danny was back. Later, I learned my friend's date wasn't a big fan of Danny; there was history there. This guy had heard some rumor about Danny in the past and was holding that against him, so he never gave Danny a chance. He acted like a jerk to Danny, and Danny wasn't going to put up with it blah-blah-blah.

After I had Danny back, and we sorted that whole situation out, Danny and I walked around the park the rest of the day like love birds, holding hands, chatting, and laughing away at everything and nothing. It looked like we were, in fact, "a thing." Maybe it was just the setting and the love stories all around us, but it seemed to be going great. We had Park Hopper tickets, so we went back and forth to California Adventure Park for the grown-up drinks and food and my favorite ride, "Soarin' Over California," then back to the Disneyland Park for "Splash Mountain." We even rode the It's a Small World ride. Yes, this big man rode the kiddie rides with me and also made fun of me all day for the fact that I was tiny and barely made the kiddie height requirement for the rides. No, I am not that short, I'm five feet, two inches; it was Danny who was tall (for me) at six feet.

"I'm wearing flip flops," I said, laughing, "of course I look short next to you, giant!" Danny loved poking fun at me, and I have never been one to stay quiet. We'd give each other a hard time and laugh like little kids. Danny had this way of making me laugh even when things weren't really that funny. We loved to people watch and make up stories of what we thought people were talking about from a distance. It was always something stupid and cheesy. The voice-over always depended on the mannerisms and facial expressions of the couples. I wonder if anyone else did that with us?

Disneyland was a success to say the least. The long day gave us an opportunity to really get to know each other more. The waiting in line for hours and little annoyances gave us glimpses into our patience levels. Overall, we had a great time. On our way home, we stopped for tacos at a little hole-in-the-wall restaurant near our house. He loved tacos—this was my kind of guy. I was really starting to like this Danny character. If you'd asked me a few weeks before if this was what I'd be doing, with this guy, the answer would have been no way! Danny wanted a relationship; I hadn't been there yet.

When Danny and I met a few months back, it wasn't love at first sight. It wasn't boy meets girl, boy asks girl out, girl says yes, and then Faby and Danny sitting in a tree K-I-S-S-I-N-G.

I met Danny while I was working in a restaurant in the South Bay, a small, very popular Mexican restaurant, Leo's Mexican food, originally family-owned since 1948. The place was a super cute hacienda-style restaurant with brightly painted colors. It had three large rooms that had beautifully hand-painted arches and was decorated in authentic Mexican décor brought from Mexico. My favorite part of the spot was the outside patio that held a beautiful Spanish-style fountain in the middle of the courtyard. It was a very quaint and family-oriented place. The owners were very pleasant to work for and I made some pretty amazing friends in my customers and co-workers. The schedule was very flexible, which I absolutely needed. I'd been working there for a few years while also bartending at a hotel in Manhattan Beach, CA, and going to school. My life as a twenty-four-year-old was very busy at the time.

Unbeknownst to me, Danny had been going to this restaurant since his high school years, and he was twenty-eight years old now, so for 10 years! I had never noticed him. I didn't even know who he was. Until one Tuesday night—I remember clearly because I was covering for a co-worker of mine—this guy in crutches and a knee brace who was dining with another guy started talking to me from across the room. I was serving them, but I honestly didn't pay attention to whom I was serving. It was late, I was tired, and I was getting ready to close the restaurant. I was sitting down at one of the tables folding napkins when I heard, "Hey, how's your night going? Busy night?"

"Um, going ok. Not really busy, Tuesday nights are pretty slow," I replied.

"You've worked here for a while, huh?"

"Yeah."

"I notice your pretty curls all the time."

"Um, thanks."

"So, what do you do when you're not working?"

Oh my gosh, can this guy stop asking so many questions? "I have an-other job, and I go to school."

"Wow, pretty busy, so no time for a boyfriend then, huh?"

"Um, no, no time for a boyfriend. Can I get you guys anything else?" I asked as I brought over their check.

"No, everything was great, thank you!" They got up and walked to the register to pay their bill.

"Thanks, have a great night," I said. It was my standard goodbye.

"See you soon," he said with a bright smile. I noticed he had a gap in between his two front teeth.

"See you soon," I said as they walked out the door. Then I closed down the restaurant for the night and headed home. To me, it had been just a normal night.

A couple weeks went by, and one night at work one of my co-workers from Leo's said to me, "There's a guy who keeps asking me for you. He's been here the last couple Tuesdays, but I've told him you don't work on Tuesdays." A guy? What guy? She went on and on about him, but I had no idea what guy she was talking about, so we moved on with our day. A few days later, this same chatty guy came in again. He tried to make small talk at first, but I noticed he wasn't the small talk kind of guy. He spoke his mind, dove right in, and asked what he wanted to ask and said what he wanted to say. He was very straightforward, and it was refreshing. I also noticed he was pretty fun-ny. Soon, we were having random conversations, and I would see him at the restaurant more and more often.

One night, he came in with his parents. Them I had noticed be-fore, I'd just never put it together that he was their son. It was a Friday night, a very busy night for the restaurant, so I had very little time to chat as he normally liked to do. They had dinner, he tried talking to me, and I was cordial—he was with his parents and it was awkward. I wasn't serving them, so I didn't feel pressured to talk. On their way out, I noticed him walking toward me as his parents headed out the door. *What is this guy doing? Why is he walking toward me?* I stood there dumbfounded, trying to figure out what he was doing with every crutch-assisted step my way. I wasn't able to run to the next room. I looked to my left and to my right hoping he wanted to speak to someone else, but he was still crutching his way to me. He had a knee brace too, so this took some time, but he finally reached me.

"Hey, when I'm less crippled, would you like to go out with me?" he asked. I couldn't help but laugh. Did he really just say that?! "Can I get your number?"

"I'm sorry, I don't date people from work," I said, "and I don't give out my number, but why don't you give me yours and I'll call you." I felt bad not giving him my number; he had crutched all this way to me, and everyone was staring.

"Ok," he said. He wrote down his number and handed it to me.

"Ok," I said, and I watched as he crutched away. I didn't know how to take it. I couldn't help but nervously laugh. *Poor guy,* I thought. He crutched all this way and now he had to crutch his way back out to meet his parents. I wanted to help him, but what could I do to help? I couldn't carry him out. Why would he ask me out with his parents waiting for him outside? *He's brave.*

The girls at work quickly wanted to know the gossip. "What did he say? Did he ask you out? Are you going to call him?"

"I don't date people from work," I said to them, "and besides, I am not dating right now. I have no time for that.

It took me five weeks to call him. One day, I was walking into work and he popped into my head. *I wonder how that guy is doing?* I thought. So, I picked up my phone and sent him a message. *Hey, it's Faby, from Leo's. How's the leg doing?*

To this he replied, *Wow! You really waited 'til I was less crippled. I'm out of town right now at Lake Nacimiento with some friends, let me call you as soon as I'm back!*

Ok, I replied, and that was that. I walked into work and went on with my day. A few days later, I got a call.

"Hey, it's Danny, crippled guy." We both laughed. He gave me a hard time for a while about me taking so long to call him. "Five weeks, it really took you five weeks?!" And he never let that go! He told me he'd looked like an idiot to his parents and the friends he'd bragged to about me. He'd been so sure I would call him right away. He'd get asked daily if I'd called, and when his answer was a no, they'd poke fun at him. "I had started to give up on you," he told me, "but I'm glad you called."

"How was your trip?" I asked.

"It was great," he said. He didn't wait long before he straight out asked, "How about a date?" This was what I had been so afraid of. I wasn't ready to date. My days were busy, and I honestly had no time between my two jobs and school.

"How about we get to know each other as friends and just hang out?" I replied.

"We can start there," he said with a smile on his face—I could tell by the tone in his voice.

"Mommy," Emma interrupted my thoughts, "we are speeding up, can you please hold my hand?"

"The plane is ready for takeoff, my love," I said as I held her hand. "Are you scared?"

"No, I'm not scared; this is exciting!" I couldn't believe this was where we were at that moment: on a plane, ready to make Emma's magical dreams come true. This was our very first trip to Disney World, for both Emma and me; I'd never been. Actually, this was our very first trip anywhere together. Emma had just turned four years old, and this trip was my gift to her. We both really needed the get-away. The last seven months had been incredibly hard, the hardest of my life. I needed a distraction. Emma needed some joy in her world. I needed and wanted to think of something else for a while. I didn't know what, but this trip was the perfect escape. Perfect except for the one thing we both wished the most, for Daddy to have been able to join us.

"Mommy," Emma said, "where's the picture of Dadda? Do you have it?"

"I do my little love, of course I have it," I replied.

"Can I hold it? I want Dadda to be with me the whole time."

★ ★ ★

Disneyworld was amazing, as magical as I had ever envisioned, except for the crazy Floridian weather that we weren't used to. It was hot and humid—nice and sunny one moment, then pouring rain the next. That's Florida for y'all. We planned this one-week Disney World trip with Chris and Jenny Hansen, their daughter Lili, who is the same age as Emma, and Jenny's mom. We all stayed at the Disney's Art of Animation Resort, they, in a Lion King themed room, and Emma and I in a Little Mermaid one, perfect for my little mermaid. The Hansens were Disney lovers and quite the experts. Thank goodness they were our guides; they definitely made this trip as wonderful as it could have been. The girls were beyond excited.

We got to see so much in the span of a week. We explored the Magic Kingdom twice, which gave us enough time for the girls to meet their favorite princesses and Minnie and Mickey, and ride all the cool rides. Emma even rode her first rollercoaster—she wasn't a big fan. Nevertheless, we had a blast. On the list was also Disney's Animal Kingdom, where we got to experience an incredible Lion King show; it was the most incredible show I had ever seen. The music and performances were so touching. The park had all the animals: giraffes, rhinos, elephants, meerkats, gorillas, and of course all the safari Disney characters, too! It was wonderful. Last, but not least, we explored the Epcot amusement park, which was magical. We visited different places of the world, including Morocco, China, Mexico, Germany, and Paris, and experienced the food, traditions, and aesthetics. The girls got their Epcot passports stamped in every country. This was the place where the idea to show Emmy the world might have started. It was magical!

I will forever be thankful to the Hansens for the friendship, support, and love they showed Emma and me. That trip wouldn't have been the same without them. To watch them hold, carry, and love Emma as they did their own daughter filled my heart; it was more than I could have ever asked for. We were missing a huge piece of us, and their generosity and kind hearts helped get us through so many difficult moments. This was, indeed, a magical trip!

Baby-mooning

Just when we gave up, the universe had a different plan for us.

We'd been married for two years when Danny and I decided we were ready to start a family. Our priorities were in order, and our married life, although not perfect, was going great. I loved this man. And he loved me. Children felt like the next big thing, a natural step in our relationship.

"Are we sure?" we'd randomly ask each other. "Let's do it!" was always the final answer. Children. I had randomly envisioned the possibility of this, but now, we were making it happen. We felt ready to become parents. "Let's get practicing on this baby thing," we'd say every night as we laughed ourselves to bed. We were young; I was twenty-seven, and Danny, thirty-one. We were perfectly healthy and eager to start a family. Life seemed to be in our favor. Everything seemed perfect.

A couple months later, we were giving some friends a ride home when I randomly smelled a popsicle that made me completely nauseous. Yes, a darn popsicle! The smell was so intense, unlike anything I had ever experienced. "Who is eating candy back there?" I asked with disgust on my face. "Can you please throw it out?!" I gave Danny a sideways look as he drove.

"I think I'm gonna throw up!" We quickly dropped our friends off at their house and headed home. "I think I'm pregnant," I said to Danny. "That was not normal, how could I possibly get sick over a popsicle?"

"Let's not get ahead of ourselves," he replied.

"I know my body, and that was not normal!"

That same night we ran over to CVS to get a home pregnancy test. "Which one do we get?" Danny asked.

"This one says six days sooner; get the box with three, just to make sure!" I replied. Once home, I ran into the bathroom and peed on the stick. I set the test carefully on the bathroom counter and sat on the toilet. *Results in three minutes*, the box said. Those were the longest three minutes of my life! Danny was patiently waiting for me in the other room when I opened the bathroom door with tears in my eyes. "So, are we? Or are we not?" I nodded and ran to him. I hugged him as hard as I could and cried on his chest.

"We are pregnant!"

The following day, I made an appointment with my OB-GYN to confirm I was actually pregnant, even though my body had been screaming at me confirming that I was. My breasts were tender, I had missed my period, and this heightened sense of smell was insanely annoying. After a blood test, it was confirmed: we were eight weeks pregnant!

"I am going to schedule an ultrasound in a couple weeks," my doctor told us, and we walked out of his office in a dream. Two weeks later we returned to my doctor's office eager to finally be able to see and hear our baby's heartbeat. Danny held my hand as the doctor put some gel on my belly and proceeded with the ultrasound wand. "Hmmm," he said, frowning, "let me try a vaginal ultrasound. Sometimes it is hard for these to pick up on such tiny beings." He proceeded with the vaginal ultrasound.

"Everything ok?" we asked as he fished for a heartbeat.

The doctor looked over at us with sadness in his eyes, "I'm so sorry, there is no heartbeat."

Danny and I looked at each other, confused. "What do you mean there is no heartbeat?"

"I am so sorry; unfortunately, you have suffered a miscarriage."

"But how? Did I do something wrong?"

The doctor explained, "It can be very common in the first twelve weeks of pregnancy to experience a miscarriage; it often occurs because the fetus isn't developing normally. I will give you both a minute."

I was in shock, and tears flowed rapidly from my eyes. "How could this be happening? Why? Why us?!"

A few days later, I was in an operating room having a D&C (dilation and curettage). I cried the entire way there and the entire way home. Danny didn't know what to say or do to make me feel better. He tried so hard to take care of me in my fragile state, emotionally and physically. "Maybe in due time we can try again?" There was hope in his voice. I wasn't sure I wanted to try again. Everything hurt.

"I don't know if I want to put us through this again!" I said.

It took my body a few weeks to recover and heal, but my heart? That was another story. I couldn't understand why this had happened to us, to me, but after much grief and processing, Danny and I decided to try again. The next time we got pregnant, we would proceed withcaution. We were fearful, unlike the first time. And just like the first time, we got pregnant pretty quickly. My body just knew. "I think I'm pregnant again, I can feel it," I said to Danny. I called my doctor with my suspicion and he asked me to come in. An in-office test confirmed that yes, I was in fact pregnant again.

We were excited, but incredibly fearful. My mind was spinning. *What if it happens again? What if I lose this baby too? What if…* My thoughts were interrupted by my doctor.

"The risk of having a second miscarriage is low, but we will keep a good eye on you; it will all be ok," he assured us.

We were cautiously optimistic, and we decided we would keep our pregnancy to ourselves until it was safe. We tried not to make too many plans, but it was difficult not to. I bought all the *What to Expect When You're Expecting* books for both Danny and myself. I studied every gestational age and development milestones. Excitement was starting to creep in. And just when we thought things were going to be ok, I got these intense sharp pains in my pelvic area, and I started bleeding. I instantly knew. I was having a miscarriage. I was alone at home. Danny was at work. I cried all by myself in the bathroom until I had no more tears left. I called my doctor and he informed me I was naturally passing the fetus. *The fetus? You mean my baby?* I called Danny and gave him the news. We were devastated. How was this happening to us again? Why couldn't I keep a baby? I obviously could get pregnant, but why did I keep losing my babies?

My doctor decided it was time to find out what was happening and performed some procedures—the most painful procedures I had ever endured. Turned out my body didn't produce enough progesterone to keep a pregnancy. The hormone progesterone is secreted during early pregnancy and prepares the uterus for housing the baby. It causes the luteal phase to start and transforms the endometrium (uterine lining) by thickening it to receive an embryo. My body never got to the thickening phase, therefore, once the embryo got to a certain gestation, my body released it. Ok, so now that we knew what was wrong with me, could we fix it?

Third time's the charm? But did we really want to put ourselves through that again? As much as I didn't, I also did. I wanted to start a family. I wanted what everyone else around me had so easily attained. People who hadn't even wanted kids had kids. Hesitantly, Danny and I decided we would try one last time. I was put on medication and was hopeful that if, when, I did indeed get pregnant again, it would be the real deal this time.

We got pregnant again, but just like the previous two times, I suffered yet another miscarriage. What was happening to my body? Was I doomed to never have children? This baby situation was taking a toll on me, my body, and our marriage. We couldn't possibly try again. Danny and I decided we would take a break from trying. It had been too much. We couldn't possibly endure any more pain.

But just when we had given up, the universe had a different plan for us. Without even trying, we got pregnant. The day we went in for our first ultrasound, we found out we were pregnant with twins. TWINS! But how? Apparently, I had gotten pregnant with a single egg, and a few days later, another egg dropped and got fertilized, too. This is called superfetation. The chances of this happening are extremely rare, but of course it happened to me. I got pregnant while already pregnant. Fraternal twins? That day we left my doctor's office in shock. *We need a bigger house!*

We felt this was the universe's way of rewarding us for all the pain we had endured. Two babies! As much as we'd wanted to, we hadn't been able to keep the news to ourselves. We excitedly told our families and closest friends. Twins! We were over the moon but also immensely scared. What if something happened? Was this too good to be true? My pregnancy was considered high risk, not only because I was carrying twins but because of my history. I was quickly put on progesterone and had weekly appointments to see my doctor. All was looking good. What if it's two girls? Or two boys? Or a girl and a boy? Danny and I had names picked out for any and all of these scenarios.

At our fourteen-week ultrasound appointment, we were eager to possibly find out the sexes of our babies, but the worst that could've happened, happened. Our worst fears were coming true. While searching for both our babies' heartbeats, my doctor could only hear one, and couldn't find a second. "I'm so sorry, I can't find baby B's heartbeat."

"Please keep looking; you have to keep looking, maybe he is hiding!" There was fear in my voice.

"I am very sorry," the doctor said. "I know you have been through so much already. This can happen sometimes in pregnancies with multiples. This is referred to as vanishing twin syndrome." *Vanishing what?* "You have experienced a type of miscarriage, usually due to chromosomal abnormality." *What happens now? What happens to the baby? What happens to my other baby? What is happening to me?*

The vanishing twin is usually reabsorbed into the placenta and into the surviving twin. "We will continue to monitor you more closely and get this baby to term. I will give you two a minute." When the doctor walked out of the office, I completely lost it. I was lying on a stupid exam table, naked, exposed, and now baby-less. Danny held me tight and tried to console me, but I was inconsolable. All I wanted to do was get out of there.

"We still have a baby in there to take care of, my love," Danny kept saying. But how could I possibly think of this baby when I had just lost my other baby?! I felt lost and confused. Grief took over me. I sat in silence the entire drive home. I cried myself to sleep for days. *What is wrong with me? Why is my body betraying me?*

Needless to say, my pregnancy was at an incredibly high risk. After a few visits to the ER, my doctor decided it was probably best that I stopped working, and he put me on complete bed rest. I was seeing my OB-GYN and a perinatologist weekly just to make sure all was going ok with the baby I was carrying. At about twenty-weeks gestation, we found out the baby I was still carrying was having complications with blood oxygen to the heart. She also seemed a lot smaller than normal for her gestational age. At our twenty-two-week appointment, we discovered our baby had severe IUGR (intrauterine growth restriction) and she had stopped growing. At this point, the perinatologist got concerned and talked to us about premature birth.

"Let's hope we can make it past the twenty-eight-week mark. The chances of survival after twenty-eight weeks are much higher."

Wait what?! The specialist advised us to take some time off, unwind, and de-stress for a few days. "This will be good for your mental health," he said. "I will see you back in a week." We left that appointment in tears yet again. Was I destined to never be a mother? Was I going to be able to carry this baby to term?

Danny decided to take the specialist's advice and booked us a quick trip to San Francisco for four days to unwind, de-stress, and spend some quality time together. This sounded nice. I couldn't remember the last time we took a trip together. Our year had been filled with so much loss and grief. Our trip to San Francisco was just what our hearts needed. We spent four beautiful days wandering the streets of San Francisco, baby-mooning, as I called it. It was wonderful.

Time

Often, we think we have all the time in the world.
Little do we know that sometimes, we don't.

May 3, 2012

11:00 am

We got to my OB-GYN's medical building in Redondo Beach. We took the shortcut, and still barely made it on time. I could never remember if it was suite 203 or 302; you would think that I'd have known that by now. I blamed it on pregnancy and pregnancy brain—it was a thing; I looked it up. I quickly went to check on the blackboard next to the elevator to confirm, 203. Not only did I have a problem with time, but I couldn't even remember where I was going. Danny used to get so irritated when we were late. "We made it, didn't we?" Eyeroll. The engineer in him was always on a tight schedule. The free spirit in me could be too relaxed sometimes.

We walked in and signed in. The receptionist handed me the pee cup, and I headed to the restroom for the routine pee sample. I came back, took a seat next to Danny, and we waited. Dr. Wu always had some children's movie playing in the office, so we watched to pass the time. Minutes later, we got called in. I could see Dr. Wu's wife in her office. She noticed me, too, and came over to say hello. She was so nice and chatty with me. She asked how I was doing, and I asked about her kids. "Wow, they are getting so big," I said.

"I'm not ready for college kids," she replied. *College*, I thought to myself. *Will I one day get to see this little peanut inside me go to college?*

The nurse sat me down, took my vitals, and walked us to exam room 1. *I like room 1*, I thought. *It has cute baby pictures on the walls.* Once we were in the exam room, Dr. Wu walked in. He looked a little more serious than normal, but I thought nothing of it. He asked how I was feeling, and I replied with an ok. Not worse than last time, but not better either. I was just bored of being on bed rest. He did a quick exam—quicker than normal—and then told Danny and me to go to Little Company of Mary Hospital in Torrance for some blood work. I was confused, why Little Company? This was not where we were delivering?

"It is closer," he'd said, "but no matter what you do, don't go home. Just go straight to the hospital from here, ok?" Like good little listeners, we followed Dr. Wu's orders and headed to the hospital, which was only minutes away. We were starving and starting to get hangry, so on the drive there we began to plan where we would go to lunch after the blood work was done.

"How about our favorite sushi place?"

"Deal, I'm sure Peter (our sushi chef) will be happy to see us and can whip me up some of his amazing preggo-friendly rolls."

12:00 pm

We arrived at the hospital and headed to the third floor, labor and delivery. *This should be quick,* we told ourselves, not thinking much of it. We got to reception and I told the nurse in charge, "Hi, we are here for blood work. Dr. Wu said you would know."

"We've been waiting for you," she said. "Do you know why you're here?"

"Blood work, we are here for blood work."

"Can you please start filling out these forms? You are being admitted," she said.

"You must be mistaken," we told her. "Can you double-check again please? We are only here for simple blood work."

"Dr. Wu will be here soon to explain," she said. Danny and I looked at each other, confused. We had so many questions, but no answers. What was going on? What was happening? Was our baby ok? *He didn't even do an ultrasound this morning!* The nurse came to tell us a room was being prepared for me and to please take a seat while they got things together. I excused myself to the restroom.

I made it to the sink and braced myself. I slowly looked up to see the girl staring back at me. She looked tired. Lost. Confused. Scared. "Don't panic, Faby," I said to myself. "Everything will be ok. Baby girl *has* to be ok. You still don't know what is happening; don't get ahead of yourself." Tears of fear started rolling down my cheeks. I quickly dried them up, fixed my hair for some reason, and walked back out to join Danny. He took my hand and squeezed it tight.

"It's going to be ok, babe," he said. "You're going to be ok."

Minutes later, the nurse handed me a blue gown and a clear plastic bag to place my belongings into. She walked us into my room and gave us some privacy so I could change. Danny helped me put on that hideous blue gown; I felt extremely exposed. Not only in the obvious you can see my butt crack kind of way, but in an emotional way too.

"Can someone explain to us what is happening? When is Dr. Wu getting here?" I was getting irritated and upset. The nurse tried to keep me calm.

"I know you must be scared, but please try and remain calm," she said as she gently helped me into bed. Once in bed, a flood of nurses, doctors, and specialists came in the room. They hooked me up to all sorts of IVs and a baby monitor, and they also placed a catheter in me.

"You are not allowed to move out of this bed, not even to use the bathroom," they told me.

Moments later, Dr. Wu finally walked in the room and explained: "You are very sick, Faby. You have what is called severe pre-eclampsia and HELLP Syndrome." *Severe what?* "Your blood pressure is extremely high and you are at very high risk for stroke or seizure. Your liver is already being damaged, and if we can't control this, your organs will start to shut down and you will start to bleed out from every pore in your body.

"But I don't feel sick," I said.

"Which is worse," he added. "In your case it is very silent. If it wasn't for our routine appointment this morning, I am not sure we would have caught this in time. HELLP syndrome is a life-threatening pregnancy complication, a more severe form of preeclampsia, and can rapidly become life-threatening for both you and your baby. Your liver enzymes are rapidly increasing which means it is severe. Left untreated, preeclampsia can lead to serious, even fatal, complications for both you and your baby, and we need to act fast." *What do you mean? I can die?!*

Dr. Wu continued, "At this point, the only way to save your life is by delivering your baby via emergency cesarean." *But my baby is still cooking inside. You can't take her out yet?! She is not ready! I am only twenty-seven weeks. Can't we wait?*

The room was spinning. I heard muffled voices in and out. *You may bleed out from every pore in your body.* Danny squeezed my hand. *Your organs will start to shut down; your liver is already at risk. We need to take this baby out. It is the only way to save your life.* The words kept echoing in my head. *This isn't happening to us, not again,* I thought to myself as the doctor kept speaking. *We just came in for a routine appointment?!* Then I heard the doctor tell Danny, "It is your baby or your wife."

I heard Danny's scared voice say, "Save my wife, please save my wife. We can always try again for a baby, but I can't lose my wife."

I was in a haze; everything was happening so fast. The doctor explained he would give me a corticosteroid shot to help with the baby's lungs. "Corticosteroids can help your baby's lungs become more mature in as little as forty-eight hours. Normally, two shots of corticosteroids are given. The first shot is administered and the other is given twenty-four hours later. It's an important step in preparing a premature baby for life outside the womb, which we know is our next step, except, we don't have forty-eight hours," Dr. Wu said.

I begged and tried to stall. *She is too tiny; she is not ready,* was all I could think. "Please, can we wait one more day so she can get the other shot?" I begged them.

"I'm sorry, we can't risk your life that long," the doctor replied.

"Please, save my baby," I begged. My voice was shaking. Tears were running down my face. My heart was pounding so strong it felt like it was trying to beat its way out of my body. Fear was getting the best of me.

"We will try our best to save you both."

I looked at Danny, who had tears rolling down his face. I don't think I had ever seen him cry like that. He was scared. I could see it in his eyes. He held me as tight as he could and wanted to say something, but the words wouldn't come out. I grabbed his face in between my hands, and I told him I was going to be ok. *We* were going to be ok. He laid his head on my chest as I always did on his when I needed comfort, and we lay in silence.

"I love you so much," he said.

"I love you too, my love."

I was scared. Not so much for myself, but for our baby, for Danny. I didn't want to lose my baby. It was a miracle I was even pregnant. We couldn't lose our baby. I collected myself and tried to play strong. "Call our parents; they will want to know what is happening," I told Danny. He went into the hallway to call them, and once I was alone, I completely fell apart. I was numb. The magnesium sulfate they were pumping into my veins to prevent a seizure was making me sick. My face had blown up like a balloon and it was making my eyes hurt. My body was declining rapidly. *I don't want to die. I don't want my baby to die. Please, God…*

Danny walked back in the room, kneeled in front of me, and we waited. Waited for answers. Waited for more tests. Waited for the medications to travel through my body and prevent the worst. Waited for a miracle. The clock was ticking. The doctor walked back in the room and told us I was still declining. "Surgery is scheduled for an hour from now." I looked up at the clock and it was 1 o'clock. *One hour. I have one hour to say my goodbyes,* I thought. *Where is everyone? Where is my mother? I need to say goodbye to my mother.*

Moments later, my parents walked in, then Danny's parents followed. They looked scared, worried, but none of us knew what to say. I remember tears, hugs, love. It was so hard to know what to do or say.

1:45 pm

It was almost time. The nurse handed Danny a surgical gown and gave him instructions on what to do. I would get wheeled into the operating room first, and once I was prepped for surgery, they would come get him to join me. Our family gathered around my bed to say one last prayer. *One last prayer.* And my life flashed before my eyes. I said goodbye through tears, and they wheeled me out.

2:00 pm

I lay in bed; big bright lights were passing fast as I looked up. My mind was racing. I was terrified. A million thoughts crossed my mind. *Will I make it out of here alive?! Will my baby survive?! Is this where my life ends? Did I really just say goodbye to everyone? What if I don't ever see them again? Do they know I love them? I hope they know how much I love them. I don't want to die. I want to be a mother. I want to be able to hold my daughter in my arms. She needs me. Danny needs me. I need you, Danny. I need you. What happens now?*

I heard two huge doors open, then shut behind me. We got to the operating room where there were about eight doctors and nurses waiting for me. *Why so many people?* I thought to myself, and as if she could read my mind, one nurse said, "Half of us are here for you and the other half are here for your baby. We have to be ready for any medical intervention; your baby will most likely have to go to the NICU." *The what?* "The Neonatal Intensive Care Unit. That is where premature and critically ill babies go to get treated and taken care of after birth." I nodded, holding back tears.

I was asked to sit up on a bed. I was helped to the bed and must have looked terrified because a really nice nurse came over to talk to me. "We will now proceed with a spinal block," she said. The spinal block procedure was explained to me: "The physician anesthesiologist will numb the area where the spinal block is administered, it may cause a little stinging or burning sensation, but you shouldn't experience too much pain. Then they will inject a local anesthetic and a small dose of morphine into the spinal fluid for pain relief after surgery." I would be numb from the level of the nipple line down but would remain awake during the birth of my baby, and Danny would be able to be present.

The nurse handed me a pillow to hug and asked me to stay very still. *I can't stay still,* I thought to myself. I was freezing and I couldn't stop shaking. I hugged the pillow tight and tried to sit as still as possible. Tears ran down my cheeks. I wasn't sure if they were tears related to physical pain, emotional pain, or fear. All I knew was I was scared and alone. *Where is Danny? When will they get Danny? I need him here! I need him here to hold my hand. I need him here for support. I need my person.*

The kind nurse tried to comfort me. She tried to distract me from the pain by talking with me. The room was suffocating. I could smell the still, sterile air. The iodine they used on my back was so strong it was starting to make me nauseous. *How did we get here?* Everything happened so fast I had no time to process. Four hours ago, I woke up to an ordinary day. And here I was now; I felt so vulnerable, naked, and exposed. The tears wouldn't stop. *I hate crying in front of people*, I thought to myself. *Why won't the tears stop? I feel like a fish out of water. I can't catch my breath. I feel so small and afraid. This is not at all how I expected I would become a mother. This is not how this was supposed to go. The fairy tales never mention this part. Why is this happening to me? Why me? There are millions of women who don't even want their babies, and us, we who have yearned for a baby with all our might can't even bring one to term?! Why is my body failing me? The one thing my body was designed to do as a woman, my body can't even do. Why is my body betraying me? Why?*

"The procedure went well, good job momma." I was snapped out of my thoughts, "Now we will prep you for surgery and go get Danny for you." *Finally, Thank You!*

They laid me down on the operating table and the anesthesiologist sat next to me. "I am here for you, to make you comfortable, so you tell me what you need ok?" he sounded so kind and gentle. *I need Danny*, I wanted to say, *I need my baby to be ok, and I need to get out of here alive*, but I just nodded. Danny finally walked in. He looked like one of the nurses in the white hospital gown and head covering. He inspected the room and looked amazed and scared at the same time. A nurse called him and handed him a stool to sit next to me.

"Hi babe," he said. Then he kissed my forehead and held my hand.

"We will get started," announced Dr. Wu, and I panicked. I wasn't positioned right. I was not comfortable. I wanted to tell someone I was not comfortable, but I couldn't bring myself to. *I can't feel my legs. I can't feel my legs.* I wanted to move my leg so badly; it was out of place. *I am uncomfortable; can someone please adjust my leg?* There was a curtain covering me from my waist down, so we couldn't see when they cut into me. Although I was numbed, I could feel them starting. My body was moving on the table.

I looked over at Danny, and he looked lost, like he didn't know what to do, or what to think or say. I tried to distract him. Then I remembered he had my camera (I always carried a camera everywhere, "just in case"). Danny would get so annoyed with my picture taking all the time, but *"You never know,"* I always said, *"I need to capture these moments."* Danny was in awe of what was happening, looking around, dissecting it all with his engineering brain, but I got his attention. I asked him to take the camera out to take pictures, so he did; he focused on that. He tried to stand to take a photo behind the curtain, but the nurse sat him down. He still managed to take a gnarly picture with my insides showing. I was glad he took that picture; I now have gruesome evidence of this moment in time.

I heard Dr. Wu say, "She is breeched," and an assistant surgeon joined him. My body was being shaken on the table; both surgeons were having a very hard time getting in there, to my daughter. They were trying not to stress her tiny, fragile little body any more than they had to because she might not have survived. They had to be very careful taking her out, so the cesarean section was more invasive than they'd planned for. A classical (upper segment, vertical, rarely done nowadays) incision of my cervix was performed while my womb incision was performed the classical bikini way (horizontal). *Talk about the pain I'll be in if I survive this!*

My mind was racing. Fear was intensifying. I couldn't focus. And I really wanted to adjust my leg. *Could someone please adjust my leg?!* Why was I so fixated on my leg? Better to focus on that than anything else happening in the room. My leg, it weighed about a thousand pounds. *Why is my body moving so much? Are they done? Is my daughter ok? Why is this taking so long? In the movies it never takes this long. Is she breathing? My leg—can someone please adjust my leg. I think I am having an anxiety attack.* I started to panic.

I looked to my left at Danny and I heard him say, "Baby girl is coming!" I looked to my right at the anesthesiologist, and he noticed fear in my eyes.

"Are you ok? What do you feel?"

"I can't feel my legs. I can't breathe," I managed to tell him. He quickly placed an oxygen mask over my face and asked me to try and breathe.

Danny looked at me, confused. "What is happening with my wife?" he asked. He sounded scared. Was it possible to be more scared? Danny didn't know whether to look at the top half of me panicking, or the bottom half of me that was being cut open and ready to show proof of life. I asked him to look at baby girl. I still couldn't breathe. I looked back at the anesthesiologist, panic in my eyes. More panic. *I don't think I can do this. I can't breathe. Am I dying?*

"She's here, a beautiful baby girl!" I heard someone say, and then everything went black.

The anesthesiologist made the executive decision to put me out.

3:16 pm

A miracle was born. Emma Isabella Ryan. 500 grams (one pound, two ounces). 10 ¾ inches.

Faby Ryan

My Miracle

*And hopefully soon enough I'll be able to see my little miracle.
The one little person I want to see with all of my soul.*

Hours after I was put out in the operating room, I woke up back in the same labor and delivery room I had been wheeled out of earlier. I was groggy. Confused. Still out of it. The medications I was on made me feel horrible and sick to my stomach. The magnesium that was still dripping through my veins made me so incredibly swollen that I felt like my skin was going to rip open from the pressure. The morphine made me confused, sleepy, and nauseous as hell. I felt disoriented and lost, but I knew I'd had a baby. I'd heard Danny say, "She's here," before they put me out.

I wanted to see my baby. *Is my baby ok? Did she live? Where is she? Where is Danny? Where am I? How long have I been out? Why am I so out of it?* I was in and out of consciousness. At one point, I remember seeing my sister-in-law at my bedside when I came to. She was talking to me, but I couldn't quite hear what she was saying, it was all muffled. I could only see her lips moving. My eyes welled up with tears. I wanted my baby. *I just want to see my baby. I need to know she's ok.* My sister-in-law was holding my hand when I suddenly got the urge to throw up. I looked around the room and there were a bunch of people there, people I hadn't seen in a while. People that hadn't been involved in my pregnancy at all.

The thing about Mexican families is, when shit happens, they will all show up, even if you haven't seen them in ages. "I have to throw up," I said to my sister-in-law. I scooched myself to the side of the bed so as not to throw up on myself, and my sister-in-law grabbed a little pink hospital throw-up bin and put it close to me. I couldn't hold it any longer, and I started throwing up uncontrollably. Then, I heard a nurse walk in. The nurse sounded irritated and concerned; she immediately asked everyone to leave the room and ran to help me. My sister-in-law said goodbye to me, and as she did, I asked her to go see my baby. I'd heard they let my parents in to see her, so maybe there was a chance they would let her and my brother see her too. I asked her to try. I couldn't see my baby, but I wanted them to. They didn't see her, though. It was late, and they had to drive back home to Bakersfield soon. Everyone else started going home, too.

I don't remember much after that. It was late, and I could see the night sky through the window. I just remember the beeping noise from the machines that gave me medications. I remember the groggy feeling, the desperation from not being able to move, and the sick feeling in my stomach. Then everything went black again.

I woke up the next morning to Danny watching over me and immediately bombarded him with questions. "How is our baby?" I asked. "Is she ok? Can I see her? When can I see her?" Due to the medication I was on, I was still not allowed to move from my bed. My blood pressure had continually been so high there were still concerns for possible seizure. Danny had been back and forth to the NICU all night. He was able to capture some pictures of our baby girl and excitedly showed me on the camera.

"Oh, babe, she's so beautiful!" he said. And I immediately burst into tears. I felt helpless. How was it that everyone else had been able to see my daughter, but I, her mother had not? Wasn't there a way to bring me to her? Or her to me? Why couldn't I see her? I could see the helplessness in Danny's face. He was trying to comfort me by showing me our daughter and there I was, a crying mess.

"She's doing ok babe; she's alive," he said. Then he continued on, giving me some medical lingo I didn't quite understand about her "sats" and oxygen levels and breathing machines and tubes. Danny was always practical, hands-on, and needed to know every detail about everything. The engineer in him was clearly present. He had already figured out all the machines and the whys behind them. He knew what every number on the monitors meant and why they beeped when they did. He was never afraid to ask questions if he didn't know something. He had also already made friends with the nurses and was calling them all by name. I admired him for how easy all this came to him. I, on the other hand, was always the emotional one; I carried my heart on my sleeve. *I feel like the worst mom ever. I should know all these things. I should be with her, too. I should be there to help comfort her. If only I would have given birth to a healthy baby. This is all my fault.* Danny held me in his arms and assured me we would be ok.

As we were having this moment, a nurse walked in with more medications. After administering them, she checked my vitals, then my incision. I was in a lot of pain and could hardly move. I was dependent solely on others for everything. As a result, I'd quickly gotten to know the nurses and staff. Danny and my mother were at my bedside most of the time in case I needed anything. They kept me company and were there in case I fell apart. I was so grateful to them. They never left me. They consoled me when I couldn't see beyond my trauma. I was an emotional mess and couldn't seem to control the random bursts of crying. My mother held me and wiped my tears; she spent sleepless night caring for and worrying about me. I was now beginning to understand the love she had for her children—her unconditional love. I would do anything to see my daughter. To love her. To hold her. To be there for her when she needed me most. It's a love that can't be explained.

The next five days were painful, literally and figuratively. I was not allowed to see my baby. I was not allowed to move. I was not allowed to eat. I was drugged. Depressed. Hormonal. An emotional mess. Family and friends got wind of the news and came by to see me. For the next five days I had visitors daily, which was nice; it helped pass the time. I felt the love. Although some days, all I wanted to do was be alone—I wanted to see no one. I was angry. Angry at myself. Angry at my body for betraying me. Angry at the situation. Angry and tired. Tired of laying in this bed. Tired of the small talk. Tired of the endless days. Tired of trying to "keep it together" and pretending like I was fine when inside I was falling apart. I felt like I was not allowed to cry because the pity comments wouldn't stop. I knew people meant well, but they didn't understand. I just wanted to see my baby. How long could a mother go without seeing her baby? Once the anger passed, though, I also felt grateful. Grateful to be alive. Grateful to have my baby still fighting. Grateful for my amazing husband who never left my side. Grateful for my mother, because when I said goodbye before my surgery, I thought I'd never see her again. But we survived. Against all odds, we survived. *And hopefully soon enough I'll be able to see my little miracle. The one little person I want to see with all of my soul.*

The evening of day five, the nurse came in and told me my

numbers were coming down; they had been steadily lowering enough that my health risks were much lower. They had already removed the catheter and decreased the medications. If all continued to go that direction and according to plan, I would be allowed to move and go see my baby. *Finally!*

I remember putting on a silky purple robe that was gifted to me by Danny's mother along with purple slippers. We never had a chance to "pack a bag" like "normal" parents get to do when they are about to deliver. Our situation was such an emergency we'd had no time for anything. We had nothing ready. Purple was not my favorite color, but it would do. I wanted to look presentable for my baby girl, so I threw on what I had. *Better than nothing*, I thought. In reality, I looked like a hot mess: my hair was up in a tangled mess of a bun, I was still incredibly swollen, and I had IV ports coming out of my arms.

I was put into a wheelchair, wheeled out of my room, and pushed around the halls until we stopped in front of the NICU doors. The nurse pressed a button on a silver keypad and someone on the other side answered, "How may I help you?"

"Mom is here for Ryan, baby girl," my nurse replied. The door buzzed and we were let in.

As soon as we were in the NICU, we went left to the wash area. Danny grabbed two little packets and handed one to me. *What do I do with this?* He opened his up and showed me a little yellow square brush-looking thing. He rolled up his sleeves, rolled mine up too, and said, "You are supposed to scrub for three minutes, from fingernails to elbows, every time you enter the NICU. This is to protect our baby from infection." I nodded.

Once we were done scrubbing, I was wheeled down a long hallway (it seemed endless to me) until we stopped in front of room 343. This particular NICU was a certified Level 3 Neonatal ICU, especially designed to care for premature and high-risk babies, and provided private single-family rooms. The room was dark and quiet, aside from the beeping of the machines. I was scared to go in. I wasn't sure what to expect or what to do. A nice nurse named Ashley welcomed me in; she was Emma's nurse for the night.

As I looked around the room, I noticed Emma's name everywhere. On a white board was the date: *Tuesday, May 8th. Emma is 490 grams today – down a few grams from last check-in. Ashley is my nurse to-day!* At the end of her plexiglass Isolette was her name, Emma, in pink construction paper with a brown hanging monkey on it; one of the nurses had made it for her. Danny wheeled me closer to the Isolette and Ashley came over to meet us. She lifted a blanket that was covering the Isolette and in there was a tiny little thing that didn't look like a baby.

She was wrapped up with blankets around her, like a barrier. Her eyes were covered with a tiny black mask and there was a huge light above shining at her. Danny proceeded to open up two little doors on the side of the Isolette so that I could put my hands through and see her. I was in shock. I had never seen anything like this. *Is this really my baby?* I have seen newborn babies before; she didn't look like a newborn baby. She was as small as the palm of my hand. Her little body was dark and see through; I could see every vein and blood vessel. Her eyes were still fused shut.

I was scared to touch her. I placed my hand on her and she moved her little arm—it was the size of my index finger. She had tape, wires, and all sorts of machines attached to her. I wanted to say hello to her, but I was scared if I opened my mouth, I would fall apart. *I have to keep it together; she can't see me cry,* I said to myself. I wanted her to feel how happy, grateful, and blessed I felt to see her, to be there with her. This felt like an out of body experience, like I was there watching someone else's story. "Hi, Emma," I said to her. "I am your mommy. I'm sorry I haven't been able to come see you, but I am here. I love you so much, baby girl."

The tears started to flow; I couldn't help them. Ashley came over to us on the other side of the Isolette and said, "I'm not supposed to, but since she's not intubated yet, I can place her on your hands for a few minutes so you can see her better."

Danny kneeled next to me and held my hand. "Yes, I'd love nothing more."

Ashley opened up the Isolette and the entire top came right up, like a capsule. It took her a few minutes to deal with all the wires, leads, oxygen cannulas, machines, and any tangles. She grabbed what looked like a bundle of hospital blankets and placed her in my arms. *Oh, my!*

"Hi there, my tiny princess, it feels so good to hold you. I've missed you so much. You're gonna be ok my little love, Mommy's here, Mommy's here." Ashley asked if we would like a family photograph and we quickly agreed. "Yes, please!" Danny handed Ashley the camera, and although not what I'd envisioned our first family photo would be, it was perfect. We were finally together, us three. That moment will forever be engraved in my heart. We sat there with our little princess in our arms, only for a few short minutes, but a few minutes was all I'd needed to keep fighting strong.

Soon after, it was time for Ashley to put Emma back in the Isolette. I didn't want to let her go. I wanted to keep her with me. I had waited so long to see her. I knew Ashley was only trying to do her job, but it hurt to let her go. It hurt to give her back. Ashley took Emma from my arms and carefully adjusted and placed her back in the Isolette. Once Emma was made comfortable and was resting, it was time to get me back to my room, too.

Danny wheeled me out of the Neonatal ICU and helped me back in bed. This was the most amazing, yet saddest night of my life. I had so many mixed emotions. I yearned to be with my daughter, yet I knew she was better off where she was. This place was saving her life. I lay in my bed, just wanting to sleep. I didn't want to think. I didn't want to feel the emptiness in my arms. I already missed my daughter so much. I had been so close to her, and now I felt so far. I wanted it to be tomorrow so I could see her again.

Motherhood

Did I really become a mother?

I'd been in this cold, sterile, sad, hospital room for five days. I'd shed more tears than I thought I had in me. I was running dry. Everything made me emotional. I had only been able to visit with my baby once, and as positive as I was trying to stay, the reality was I was not in a good place. I was missing feeling like a mother. I was missing my child. I was missing the one thing I had been admitted into this hospital for: Motherhood.

"Welcome to motherhood," I was told. Motherhood, what a strange concept that was for me. I didn't feel like a mother. I hadn't felt like a mother yet, not throughout my pregnancy, and not now. Now felt like a rollercoaster of emotions I wasn't sure how to navigate. Now was full of pain and trauma I hadn't prepared for. The *What to Expect When You're Expecting* books never mentioned anything about emergency surgeries, micro-preemies, or Neonatal Intensive Care Units. The books I'd read had only talked about fetuses the size of fruits at specific week gestations and had only described in detail the beauty in which they were developing. These books never mentioned what would happen if that "fruit" was born before its time. I delivered Emma at twenty-seven weeks gestation, but because she'd had severe IUGR by about four weeks, she had been born the size of a twenty-three-week-old fetus. At twenty-three weeks, the books tell you, your baby is as big as a grapefruit. The average twenty-three-week fetus measures 11.4 inches from head to foot and weighs 1.1 pounds. My baby was born the size of a grapefruit, 1.125 pounds and 10 ¾ inches long. Have you ever held a grapefruit in your hand? This was the size of my baby at birth.

What the books also don't tell you is that babies born after only twenty-three to twenty-four weeks are so small and fragile that they often do not survive. Their lungs, heart, and brain are not ready for them to live outside the womb without extreme medical intervention and treatment. The traditional baby books don't tell you that there is a chance your baby might not survive (seven out of ten die) and in the chance that they do survive, there is also a chance that treatment will cause your baby suffering and harm. *Suffering and harm—we were already experiencing suffering and harm.*

My baby looked more like an experiment than a baby: Machines were attached to her body from whichever angle you looked at. She was being poked, probed, and prodded every five seconds. I'd heard terminology I didn't understand, medical terminology I had only heard in shows like *ER* and *Grey's Anatomy*. I felt more like a stranger to my daughter than a mother. A visitor. An onlooker. This was not motherhood. Motherhood to me did not look nor feel like what I'd seen with most mothers I knew. From what I'd known, these women had gotten pregnant, and nine months later, boom, a healthy baby got to come home; the whole world comes and showers and celebrates said child. Why couldn't this be me? Why couldn't I bring a healthy baby home and be showered like the rest? I didn't even get to have a baby shower! Stupid I know, thinking about baby showers, but I got cheated out of every beautiful experience that comes with having a baby. Would I ever be able to experience bringing home my baby? *What if she never gets to come home? What if… I don't even want to finish that sentence.*

The day after I met Emma for the first time, five days after she was born, I was told I was getting discharged. I was going home. I was going home without my baby. Empty-handed. Nothing ever prepares you for this. Nothing ever prepares you for the empty feeling inside, the overload of sadness, guilt, and anger that overtakes you. This was not the way it was supposed be. This was not how motherhood worked! I felt miserable. Little. Ripped off. Not only was I already full of hormones, emotions, and feelings of guilt for not being able to bring a healthy baby into the world, but now I was leaving this hospital empty-handed. I was leaving my sick, fragile, barely surviving baby behind. *What kind of mother does that?! What kind of mother am I?!* I was angry at myself. I failed Emma as a mother.

I was dreading getting discharged. Not because I didn't want to go home—of course I wanted to go home. I just didn't want to go home without my baby. Staying in the hospital meant I was closer to her in proximity, just around the hallway, on the same floor, in the next unit, just a few doors down. Getting discharged meant I'd be far from her, miles from the hospital, further away than I ever wanted to be. The fact that I couldn't be close to my daughter and hold her any time I wanted, like a "normal mom" was already excruciating, but the thought of going home and not being close to Emma was more than I could handle. Discharge paperwork had already started, so it was only a matter of time, but I wasn't ready to go.

The kind nurse that wheeled me out of the hospital asked if I wanted to be wheeled out through the back where I wouldn't run into other new moms also getting discharged and leaving with their newborn babies in their arms. She thought this would add to my heartache and she wanted to help ease my pain a little by avoiding any and all trace of happy moms and happy, healthy, beautiful newborn babies. I agreed. The last thing I wanted to do was watch as other mommies were happily wheeled out with their perfect new babies. I felt envious, ripped of the experience. So, I was wheeled out through the back elevators and doors to the hospital, like a ghost, invisible, with empty arms. A new mom without her baby.

I felt broken. I was broken, literally and figuratively. I was in so much pain, not just emotional but physical, too. With every floor down, the pain intensified. I was further and further away from the little being I'd given birth to just days before. The pain from my c-section also reminded me of this; with every movement, my insides felt like they would rip open any minute. My body was still swollen from all the medication. I felt like a giant balloon, over-stuffed with air, about to pop. I did not look or feel like myself. The doctors hadn't been able to fully control my blood pressure yet; it was still high. The medication was taking long to bring it down to normal; it would take time. I felt horrible and had an insane headache.

I looked to Danny for comfort; I just wanted him to hold me and tell me all would be ok, but when I looked at him, he also looked worried. Distressed. I know he was also trying to keep it together. I didn't want to add to his load because he was already so busy trying to get everything together and into the car: my meds, my things, all sorts of flower arrangements, balloons, and loving gestures from family and friends. His hands were full. The nurse and volunteer walking with us looked at me with loving, but worried eyes. I tried not to make eye contact. I tried so hard to hold my tears. I didn't want to fall apart. But how was I supposed to feel when everything was so fucked up? My baby was upstairs in the NICU fighting for her life and here I was leaving her behind. I tried to keep it together, but the lump in my throat was growing bigger and bigger. I felt fragile. Suddenly, the tears just flowed; I couldn't stop them. I tried. I just wanted everything to be ok. I wanted Emma to be ok. I wished I had a magic wand that would fix it all. Where was fairy godmother when you needed her? I was falling apart. I felt drained, drained in every which way, but I needed to get it together. If I fell apart, I didn't think I could be put back together. I had to be strong for Danny, for Emma, for all of us.

The car ride home was quiet. I stared out the window the entire time. The early May sun was hitting my face through the window. I could see flowers starting to bloom as we drove through the streets. I couldn't look away. I couldn't look at Danny. I couldn't say a word. Everything hurt. Danny held my hand the entire time and squeezed it every so often as if to remind me to breathe. "I love you babe," he said. "Everything is going to be ok; our little monkey is going to be ok. We will call the NICU as soon as we get home to check in on Emmy, and I will bring you back in the morning. You just need to get some rest tonight, ok?" I nodded. Tears streaming down my face as I looked out the window.

The last time I'd been home was the morning before our world suddenly turned upside down, before my body failed and betrayed me, before I went into surgery. I couldn't even remember how I'd left our house. *Did I clean the house before we left? Did I even unpack?* The day before our life-changing appointment, we had just gotten home from our four-day "baby-moon" trip to San Francisco after our very difficult few months with the loss of our twin and the series of complications during my pregnancy. I couldn't remember if I'd done anything at home. As fast and sudden as everything happened, time seemed to stand still. Everything seemed like it happened so long ago. It felt like years since I'd been home. Emma's nursery wasn't even ready yet. Nothing was ready. I wasn't ready. My baby was definitely not ready. I walked into the house and everything felt strange. The Faby that had walked out of this house days before was no longer recognizable. I'd changed. Everything had changed. I opened the door to Emma's nursery and instantly broke down. Everything was wrong. Motherhood was not supposed to start this way. *A mother without her baby is no mother at all. Did I really become a mother?*

★★★

Pregnancy, motherhood, the road to motherhood didn't come easy for me as it does for many others. You see, motherhood comes in different shapes and sizes. Some of us wish for motherhood with all our might. We yearn to be mothers more than anything else in the world. Some of us lose our motherhood with our losses, as I did after four miscarriages and the loss of my daughter's twin. For some of us, the trauma and the pain to get to motherhood is too grand. And some of us, are never able to get there.

Baby-less

*Strength is found in surviving the journey
we have absolutely no control over.*

May 9, 2012

The day we got home from the hospital, baby-less, broke me. All the strength I had been trying to grasp on to, for Danny, for our families, for myself even, vanished. I felt helpless. Empty. Lost. I sat in our empty nursery for hours until Danny dragged me out of there. "You have to get some rest, my love. How about I make you some food?"

I wanted nothing. Absolutely nothing. Nothing but my baby. "Let's call the NICU and check in on how Emmy is doing. Will that make you feel better?" Knowing Emma was ok was the only thing that made me feel better, that allowed me to breathe.

"Hi, this is Faby Ryan calling for Ryan baby girl. How is Emma doing? Who will be her nurse tonight? Can I get her stats?"

"Let me transfer you to her nurse."

"Hi, how is Emma doing since we left? Did she go up any grams?" (In the NICU, everything is measured in grams, and every gram counts.)

"She's gone down a few grams, but it is normal for preemies to lose a little weight. She will adjust and will start going up in weight." At one point Emma weighed less than a pound.

"Has she had any episodes?"

"No episodes since you left, Mom."

An episode, or bradycardia, is when the heartrate slows down, usually to less than 80 bpm for a preemie. A lot of times, bradycardia happens after apnea (forgetting to breathe) or periods of very shallow breathing. Emma's chest would contract, and she would stop breathing constantly.

"How is she breathing?"

"Her breathing is ok; she is resting."

How can she be ok and resting when I'm not there? I should be there taking care of her, not you!

"I am glad she's happy and resting, thank you. How's she doing with the oscillator vent?"

An oscillator vent is high-frequency oscillatory ventilation; it's typically used when conventional mechanical ventilation fails. Oscillator vents can improve oxygenation when they're used early on, and they are gentler modes of lung ventilation. This is especially good for neonatal lungs because oscillator vents reduce ventilator-induced lung injuries. Unlike traditional ventilators, which essentially inflate and deflate the baby's lungs like a set of billows, the oscillator keeps the lungs open with a constant positive end-expiratory pressure and vibrates the air at a very high rate (up to 600 times per second). While mechanical ventilation came with high risks, it was our only option. Because of Emma's extremely underdeveloped lungs, the oscillator was the best way to give her lungs a fighting chance with less long-term damage.

"Has she pulled her tube off again? What do her numbers read?"

"Not since the last time we talked. Please tell her not to do that anymore. She likes to keep us on our toes!" Emma, the little fighter she was, loved pulling her breathing tube out any chance she got and would freak the NICU (and us) out! She was starting to show those doctors and nurses who was boss!

"What's her heart rate?" Preemies tend to have faster heart rates than full-term babies. In general, a heart rate of 120-160 beats per minute is normal for a preemie and 80-140 beats per minute for a full-term baby.

"Has she had a desat?"

"She's had a few, but nothing to worry about, Mom, she is ok." A desat is when the heart slows down in response to the low blood oxygen levels. Together, apnea and bradycardia are often called "spells" and a low blood oxygen level is often called a desaturation, or desat for short.

"What does her pulse oximeter monitor read?" Pulse Oximetry is a non-invasive method for monitoring a person's blood for oxygen saturation. It's a vital instrument in the care of infants in the NICU

"Her numbers are stable, Mom."

"What did her blood gas say today?" A blood gas is an arterial blood test that measures oxygen and carbon dioxide levels in the blood. The test can show blood PH levels and lung function and can help the doctor determine how well the lungs and kidneys are working. This test is often used in acute situations to help diagnose the cause of breathing difficulty. Emma had daily blood gas tests.

"No results yet, but we'll let you know as soon as the lab brings them up."

"Is the blood transfusion working?"

"Dad is a hero; she is taking the blood transfusion very well." Emma needed an emergency blood transfusion, and without hesitation, Danny gave our baby girl his blood. Luckily, a perfect match. I wished I had been able to, but with my condition, I hadn't been an option. This transfusion was saving her.

"Has her PDA closed? Are the meds working?" PDA, or Patent Ductus Arteriosus, is a heart defect caused by problems in the heart's development. It is an abnormal opening between two blood vessels, the aorta and the pulmonary artery, leading from the heart, which causes increased blood flow to the lungs and strains the heart. After birth, the ductus arteriosus normally closes within 2-3 days, but in preemies, the opening takes longer to close. When the connection remains open, it is referred to as a patent ductus arteriosus. PDA is twice as common in girls. *Lucky us!* A doctor will usually diagnose PDA after listening to the child's heart. Most cases of PDA cause a heart murmur (an extra or unusual sound in the heartbeat). A small PDA may cause no symptoms, but a large one can allow poorly oxygenated blood to flow in the wrong direction, weakening the heart, and causing failure to thrive, or breathlessness. It is important to correct a PDA because it can lead to congestive heart failure and a disease of the right side of the heart later in life.

Emma's PDA was on the large side. She was in treatment to try and get it to close with medication, but so far it wasn't working as well as we hoped. It was all a waiting game. A game I never wanted to play.

Was this my fault too? Did I pass this on to my daughter?! I, too, was born with a heart murmur.

"Any other new meds?"

"Not for now, Mom."

"Has she been taking her bolus feeds ok? Did you have enough breast milk for today? We can come drop off more later tonight."

Because Emma wasn't able to feed by mouth, she had an NG (nasogastric) tube, which carries food and medicine to the stomach through the nose, placed in.

The nurses and I were astounded at the fact that I had developed even the slightest bit of breast milk. Since Emma was born so early, no one expected me to produce any, but now we all saw it as liquid gold. If there was the slightest chance that I could produce and help my baby in any way, I definitely would. I wasn't getting much, really, maybe an ounce every couple hours, but to me, every milliliter was a blessing.

"She is tolerating the feeds ok; we might up them a few cc's, even." Emma was only receiving a mere 5-10 cc's at a time because it was all her little body could handle.

"Thank you, we will come by tonight once rounds are given."

"See you then, Mom. Don't forget to also take care of yourself."

"Don't worry about me, I'll be fine; I just want baby girl to be ok."

We learned so much of the lingo that came with having a micro-preemie. Danny and his engineering mind, always wanting to know how everything worked, came in so handy. He was teaching me all he'd learned over the five days I was so sick I hadn't been able to see Emma. He'd definitely stepped up to the plate; such a good, hands-on, and proud daddy.

Our calls to check on our baby girl were more informational and "doctor-like" than "parent-like." You see, life for us as "NICU parents" was more complicated than we'd ever thought. There was so much we were forced to learn, and yet, so much more we still had to learn. Checking in on our baby girl wasn't as simple as, "How's baby girl doing?" It was a world beyond anything we had ever imagined—scary to say the least, and full of uncertainty. We were holding our breaths between every call to the NICU. Things could change any minute, so every second counted. Bringing baby home was a distant thought. Making sure baby was alive on the hour was how we lived.

As much as Danny wanted me to rest that night, I couldn't. The pain of my c-section was killing me and my blood pressure was still high, unable to get under control. I wasn't me. And all I wanted to do was to see my baby. So, we did the next best thing we knew to do. At

8:00 pm, Danny carried me into the car, and to the hospital we went. The 4.8-mile car ride from home in El Camino Village to the hospital in Torrance, CA, was quiet, except when the bumps on the road made my insides feel like they were about to split open. I held my hands to my stomach tight thinking that if I held tight enough, my insides wouldn't fall out into the car. Against my better judgement, I had put on one of those stupid recommended girdles for c-section recovery. I instantly regretted it; it pinched and made me hurt more than it gave me relief.

After the most painful car ride, we'd finally arrived at the emergency entrance to Little Company of Mary Hospital, the hospital I left my baby-girl in all alone. The emergency entry was the only way to get to the NICU after hours, so Danny went in, grabbed a wheelchair, and wheeled me in. "Hi, what's your emergency?" they asked.

"We are here for the NICU. Our baby girl is up there!"

"You'll need to sign in here and get a bracelet." We did. The corridor from Emergency to the inner part of the hospital was long and confusing. In a panic, it was easy to get lost. We got lost.

"It's ok, babe, we will find our way," Danny assured me. And by the grace of the hospital gods, we found a nurse that led us to the elevators, and up to the third floor. I kept quiet and looked up at Danny every so often. I felt so confused and out of place and wondered if he did, too. Danny was always so confident and could figure his way around any scenario, no problem; I envied him. I had been so scared and so lost. I felt little, and I saw him as this big, amazing being taking care of me and our baby girl. I wished I could be more like him: Strong. Confident. Healthy.

"Parents of baby girl Ryan," we said as we buzzed in.

"Come on in." I was learning the routine. Walk into the washroom, sleeves up. Remove any jewelry, scrub for three minutes, and walk (or wheel me) down the hallway to room 343. One of the comforting things I found with this hospital was the fact that Emma had a private room. I was in no shape to be around people, and this at least gave me a little privacy to look as lost, shocked, or scared as I felt without anyone thinking I was a shitty mom (just how I saw myself and my body that betrayed me).

"Hi Mom and Dad, Emma is well and resting," the nurse said as

Danny wheeled me in next to the incubator. She then followed with a full report on our daughter's stats.

"Hi, little love, Mommy is here!" I looked over at the nurse. "Can I touch her?"

"Of course, just be very gentle." I wanted so badly to feel like a mom. I wanted so badly to feel "normal." But what the hell was normal when I was looking at my baby through an Isolette and asking a nurse for permission to touch my own daughter?! How could I possibly feel like a mom? Nothing about this was normal! I sat there in a wheelchair, staring at my tiny little bird of a daughter, hoping she could feel me, hoping she could hear me. Her eyes were still fused shut and covered with a black mask. The monitor over her Isolette went off, beeping like crazy, numbers flashing red and green. I freaked out. The alarms and machines warned of something wrong.

"What is happening to her?" I panicked. *Did I do something wrong?* The nurse then asked me to put my hand over her, which covered her entire body.

"She feels comforted this way. She can feel you." As I placed my hand over her, immediately, the stats on the monitor settled. I felt her body relax. *She can feel me. She knows I am here. She knows I'm her mommy.* Tears streamed down my face. *I love you, little love, I love you so much!*

That night I went home knowing my baby knew who I was. I loved her more than I had ever loved any other little human. And I made it my mission to never fail her. To be there for her day and night. To learn all I had to, to be her biggest advocate. I would fight for her the way she was fighting for me. I knew it wouldn't be easy—nothing about our journey together had been thus far, but she was here, alive.

May Flowers

Without rain, there would be no flowers, or rainbow babies.

The following day, Thursday, May 10, 2012, Mexican Mother's Day, would be my first Mother's Day. It's a day that is celebrated hugely in my culture and in my family, regardless of American Mother's Day. For us, it was always twice the celebration. But then, it was a day I dreaded. I didn't want to be celebrated. How could I celebrate when my baby wasn't with me? Who celebrates a mother without her child?

I woke up in a daze. Exhausted. I was pumping my breasts every two hours as directed by the lactation specialist, only to get a couple ounces the entire night. Plus, we accidentally spilled some of it. My breasts were engorged, milk-less, sore, and dry. I was mad at them. Whoever said "don't cry over spilled milk" obviously had no idea what they were talking about. When you're a micro-preemie parent, you cry over everything! Spilled milk and Mother's Day was definitely at the top of the list of reasons to cry that day. Fortunately, to my surprise, and contrary to what I thought I wanted, my incredibly thoughtful mother came over with a beautiful sunset-colored flower arrangement: red roses, orange orchids, and peach carnations all beautifully assembled in a brown basket. "From Emmy, to Mommy, Happy First Mother's Day" the card read. My heart filled with love. It was all worth it. This would all be worth it. *Emma has to be ok, she just has to.*

Days went on and turned routine. Pump all night, every two hours. Wake up at 7 am, call the NICU to get Emma's stats. Be in the NICU by 8 am, after rounds. Spend the day with Emma. Go home between 5 and 6 pm. Call the NICU to get Emma's stats. Go back to the NICU with Danny after he was off of work—8 pm. Go home by 10-11 pm. Repeat.

Danny went back to work after taking a couple weeks off to take care of me as we adjusted to our new routine, so I spent a lot of my time alone—mostly in the hospital. The hospital valet and the cafeteria employees all knew me by name. "Hi, Mrs. Ryan," they'd say as I pulled up to the hospital. "How is Emma today?" Emma was one of the tiniest babies this NICU had ever had, so her story had been heard by many. These people had become my friends, my familiar faces.

After considering our options, Danny and I decided it made sense for us to break up his paternal paid leave, which was twelve weeks here in California. He would go back to work for the time being, and we would use his remaining paternal leave when Emma was ready to come home from the NICU. This way we could both bond, take care of, and spend time with our little love once she was home to make up for lost time. It had been a hard decision since all I wanted was for us to do this together. I wanted him to be by my side, to be my support system as I sat daily with our tiny baby, but it wasn't practical financially. Also, his role at his job was crucial at the time. He had a huge project he'd been leading, and a lot of people depended on him. Sacrifices. More sacrifices that needed to be made.

Another week went by; I was beginning to heal from my high blood pressure and my cesarean incision, which was incredibly painful and took longer than expected to heal. I was finally able to get around without the assistance of a wheelchair in the NICU, which made my trips there a little easier. I was healing physically, but mentally and emotionally, I was a mess. As close as we were, I felt like Danny didn't quite understand the emotional pain I was going through. He mostly only saw my physical pain, which he could help fix and was starting to heal, but he couldn't really see the damage all this had done inside of me.

"How can you possibly think this is your fault?" he asked. "Maybe try and stay home a little more and rest. Don't stay in the hospital so long." It was hard for me to explain to him the mom guilt and the anger at my body for betraying me. "But none of this is your fault, babe," he said again and again. Oh, but to me it was. This was all my fault. Our daughter fighting for her life daily was all my fault. The logic in him couldn't understand all this guilt and pain, but emotional me was dying inside. I couldn't explain to him in a way he fully understood.

Danny was incredibly supportive, but it was different for him. He wasn't living inside me or the chaos in my head. In addition to the chaos, my days were consumed by my twelve-hour hospital shifts. The only human interactions I had were the NICU nurses, the cafeteria staff, and family and friends when they were able to come sit with me during the day, which was impossible for most because everyone else had a life while my life was inside a hospital. Danny went back to work, to a semi-normal, social life, and I was stuck in my grief, pain, and daily solitude with our baby fighting for her life. I kind of resented his semi-normalcy. I understood why he had to go back to work logically, but again, the emotional me was a mess and was drowning. Our life was on autopilot, and it felt like we were driving two separate cars. I hated this feeling.

I didn't want to add strain to our marriage on top of everything else. I was afraid we wouldn't survive it. We were so fragile at that time and in survival mode. I tried so hard to be strong, to eat my feelings and shove them in as deep as possible to keep them all hidden from Danny, but my face has never been in sync with my heart. My feelings have always shown right through. "Certain life situations either make you or break you," Danny used to say, and I wasn't about to let this break us. We had to be a team at all costs; this was the only way we could survive this journey. So, I braved up, poured my heart out as I cried like a baby, and asked for help.

★★★

I didn't know this at the time, but everything I was experiencing—my feelings of guilt, anxiety, inevitable crying spells—was postpartum depression. Back then, I didn't even know this was a thing. No one had ever talked to me about it. I always thought my feelings were new mom "baby blues" and the obvious sadness of having a baby in the hospital fighting for her life. What I was feeling was unlike anything I had ever felt before. It was beyond my control. There were never-ending sadness and crying spells even when I wanted to feel grateful and strong. I couldn't sleep. I couldn't eat. Everything annoyed and irritated me. I pulled it together until I couldn't anymore more. And even that made me sad. The guilt of my body's betrayal was killing me inside. This was a never-ending daily cycle that went on for months, years. But I just dealt with it. I didn't know any better. I wish I would have known then what I know now and had looked for help. I wasn't a terrible mother. I was going through so much. It was all so incredibly overwhelming, and I didn't have the tools at the time to help myself.

If you are a new mother and feel any of this, please look for help. Don't allow these feeling to consume you. Do know it is *not you*, it is an illness. And there is help out there for you. It is treatable. There are professionals who can guide and help you. You are not alone.

★★★

In the NICU, we were introduced to Lisa Pedersen, a clinical social worker and counselor for the unit. Her job was to support families of patients in the NICU and help them walk the intense, life-altering journey together as the day-to-day rollercoaster of having a critical baby in the NICU unfolded. Our first meeting with Lisa was incredibly intimidating; it was in an office setting, but we could tell she tried to set it up as an inviting and calm environment. Her personality was just that, very calm and inviting.

She offered drinks and snacks, but the last thing I wanted to do was have a snack. I wanted her to fix me and tell me why I couldn't stop blaming myself for my daughter's current situation. I wanted her to tell me that resenting Danny's semi-back-to-normal life outside of me didn't make me an asshole, and that we were still a team. I wanted her to tell me she had seen other families in our situation and that those babies had survived and gone home, healthy. I wanted affirmation that we would be ok. So I sat there, staring at everything and nothing.

Danny, on the other hand, opened up right away. He was not the shy, hesitant type. He filled Lisa in on Emma's situation and that made her smile, not our situation, but him opening up and talking so sweetly about our tiny baby and his experience as a new father. We weren't the only ones invited to this meeting. Two other couples with babies in the NICU had also joined, and I was eager to hear their stories to see if maybe (but sadly) we did have something in common. I wanted to feel less alone. I needed to feel that someone else understood and felt what I was going through. Unfortunately for me, but fortunately for them, their babies were in a less critical situation than ours and would be going home soon enough. I was incredibly relieved for them, of course; no parent should ever have to see their baby suffer, not even for a day, but this did make me feel even more alone.

We met with Lisa weekly. We talked about Emma's health and where we were in the process, and slowly, I started to open up and share any and all feelings I had about Emma's diagnosis, our family life, and Danny and myself as a unit. We soon looked forward to talking to Lisa. We learned she loved to use the word "yummy" as a reference to a feeling. "What makes you feel yummy inside?" she would ask. Seeing Lisa was definitely starting to help, but I always felt like I was missing something. I wanted to talk to and reach out to other parents of micro-preemies—only they could really understand what I was going through—but I had an incredibly difficult time finding other families we could relate to.

This was a time when social media wasn't what it is now; it wasn't as open and educational on subjects like these. I barely knew how to work Instagram or Facebook, and I only used them to update family and friends on Emma's medical condition. With nothing else other than hospital life going on, I made it my purpose to research and find other parents of micro-preemies. I would spend nights looking up Emma's diagnosis and roaming web pages I could find on these tiny miracles. The first and only page I found at the time was grahamsfoundation.org. I read their story and messaged them, and they were kind enough to send a little care package to my home with a beanie, some bracelets, and a video. They were building a community of preemie parents and I wanted to know more. One day, I hoped to be able to do the same for someone else.

This journey hadn't been and wouldn't be any easy one—this we were already learning. We had a long road ahead, but we would pull through, together. One day at a time became our motto. We knew so much yet so little. And just when we thought we had a small handle on things, life threw us another curveball.

Resilience

She wasn't a perfectly healthy baby, but she was just perfect for us.

Emma Isabella Ryan, 23 days old. 680 grams.

After two rounds of edication, Emma's PDA hasn't closed. Emma needs heart surgery stat! Surgery is scheduled for May 29, 2012.

I wasn't able to sleep at all the night before Emma's scheduled surgery. *How can they operate on her? She is so tiny, merely a pound-and-a-half!* The idea of them cutting into our little girl's body was more than this already scared and fragile mother could take, but if they didn't perform the surgery, we might have lost her. Dr. Jon, one of Emma's doctors and director of the NICU, assured us that Dr. Ndiforchu, the surgeon, was the best and that Emma was in great hands. They explained she would be put under general anesthesia and they would be going in through her back. *Her back? I've never heard of such a thing! How?* They would make an incision on the left side and through her ribs to reach the PDA, then they'll place a titanium clip to close it. *So, she will have a metal clip in there for the rest of her life? What if the surgery doesn't work? What if she can't withstand the surgery? What if…*

"Try and relax, Mom and Dad, she is in great hands," Dr. Jon said. The NICU had a surgery room they used for critical situations, so the surgery would be done on the same floor. Transferring Emma to another surgical floor would have been too much for her.

"Mom, would you like to help assist with her transfer? This will give you an opportunity to hold her for a few minutes while doing so." My heart filled at the idea of getting to touch and hold my little girl, if only to assist.

"Of course I would; I would love that very much!"

The following morning, we arrived at the NICU hopeful and terrified. *This surgery can save our baby's life. But this surgery can also kill her.* I tried not to think of the latter. I tried to stay positive. I talked to all of Emma's nurses, asking for their expertise and experience on the matter. They all assured us this was the right decision that could help Emma thrive. I held on to the healing vibes sent to us by everyone who knew what we were going up against. I had faith in Emma, her doctors, the surgeon, and her medical team. There were nonstop prayers sent our way. I wanted to believe so much that our faith and what I believed in would carry us through. My mom, dad, sister, and Danny's dad and stepmom all came with us for support. They waited in the parent lounge while we went in to see our little love. Upon entering, we saw Emma's room was filled with her medical team: NICU director, neonatologists, respiratory therapists, and nurses, and then there was us. It took eight people to help us transfer Emma from her Isolette to the travel Isolette she needed to get to the surgery room where another team of surgeons and medical assistants would be waiting for her.

"Ok, Mom and Dad, here is the plan: we are going to disconnect Emma from the breathing machine and bag her (or manually ventilate) and place her on your chest for a few minutes so you can give her some love before we settle her into the travel Isolette and take her into surgery where they will prep her the rest of the way." I looked like a deer caught in the headlights and just nodded. I was incredibly scared; I did not want to hurt her or damage anything. She was connected to leads, IVs, and wires through every open space on her tiny body. They had run out of veins to use on her fragile body (most of them were blown from so much use) that they even had to place one of the IVs, which was being used for antibiotics to prevent any infection, on her head. She looked so tiny and so fragile in the center of it all; she must've been as scared as I was.

The team picked her up from her Isolette as carefully as possible, wires now attached to all sorts of portable machines. I held my breath the entire time as the team helped me place her on my chest, and then, there she was, lying on Mommy, fragile and tiny, hugging me with her tiny little arms that perfectly laid on my chest. Her entire body laid in between my breasts, her head was on my clavicle, and her legs fell just above the bottoms of my breasts. When I looked down, my chin touched the top of her head. She looked lifeless and tired. I tried to hold back my tears, but a magnitude of feelings and emotions were running through me. *I love you so much, baby girl, you have to pull through for us. You have to fight, my little love, you just have to.* I kissed her head as her respiratory therapist continued to bag her behind me, everyone was watching me as well as all the monitors to make sure she was doing ok. Danny came up beside me and caressed her too, giving her kisses on her tiny head. *We love you, Emmy; please, you have to make it through this.* We snapped a few photos of this moment, not wanting to let go, but soon it was time for us to give her back. With the help of the medical team, I laid Emma in the travel Isolette. I gave her one last kiss, and I said goodbye to my little love. The medical team rushed her out of there, and there we stood, Danny and I, unsure if we would ever see our baby girl alive again.

Danny and I went back to the waiting area on the NICU floor to meet our family. The room silenced as we walked in. "How did it go? How is she?" they all asked.

"They just took her in; she has to pull through, she just has to." I sat in a corner of the room in a lounge chair; my breasts were ready to explode, and I needed to pump my breastmilk. Danny asked Lori, one of Emma's nurses for a Medela pump, which I normally used when I needed to pump while in hospital, and she graciously brought one to me. I sat there, my heart aching, and pumped away. Time traveled in slow motion. We asked Lori, who would be in the surgery room, to please keep us updated as best she could, and she did just that. After some time, she came out with an update.

"Emma had a little episode. She might have gotten a little too much anesthesia and she clamped down for a second, but she is doing fine now."

"What do you mean clamped down?" we asked.

"She spasmed for a second. It can happen, but she is ok."

My heart literally stopped. "So you mean she stopped breathing on the operating table?"

"Don't worry, Mom and Dad, she is ok. Everything is looking good now; I have to go back in there. I will come back with another update as I have one."

As if I hadn't already been worried enough, this sent me over the edge. I couldn't breathe. I wouldn't be ok until I knew everything had gone well and my baby was out of surgery. I couldn't even tell you how much time went by because for me it felt like an eternity, but some while later, Lori came back with more updates.

"Emma is out of surgery. All went well, and the doctor will come talk to you shortly once Emma is well and resting."

"Thank God! When can we see her?"

"Once she is back in her room and resting."

The time between the last update and us being able to see our daughter felt endless, but we were finally able to see her. She was laying on her tummy as her incision had been done through her back, and there was white surgical tape covering the surgical site.

"Hi, little love, Mommy and Daddy are here," I said to her as tears were streaming down my face. "You pulled through, little love. You pulled through, my little fighter!" We sat next to our daughter for a long time, watching her breathe, hoping she could feel us. Then Dr. Jon came in the room.

"Everything went well in there. We weren't able to fully close her PDA—it remains a little bit open—but with time, it should fully close on its own; it shouldn't affect her." We nodded, emotionally drained. At this point, we were just glad our baby survived the surgery. We would have to take it one day at a time and hope that with time, she would gather more strength to keep fighting.

On June 9th, our baby officially met the two-pound mark, and we celebrated such a huge milestone. In the NICU, and for micro-preemies, every ounce counts. Every month after that, a new pound was gained, slowly but surely. On July 11th, sixty-nine days after Emma was born, I was able to hold and kangaroo (hold with skin-to-skin contact) my baby for the first time. I had so long awaited patiently for this moment, trying to stay as positive as I could, trying in every other way to be there for her: changing diapers, taking temperature, doing bolus feeds, watching as they bathed her in a tiny pink hospital bin, tirelessly trying and hoping to breastfeed her, but no matter what I did, I hadn't felt like a real mom. But now, the day had come when I would finally get to hold her, and she would be able to feel my love.

Emma's nurse and respiratory therapist helped make the magic happen. I sat in a lounge chair wearing a hospital gown as they pulled her out of her Isolette. They carefully arranged all of the wires and machines in place so that she could easily lie on my chest. And then, the best moment in the world happened: I got to hold Emma for the first time, like a real mother, skin-to-skin. There was tape up and down my gown holding her breathing tube in place, leads coming off of me, and her NG tube carefully taped back. It was an entire process, but I didn't care. I was finally holding my baby. *Hi, Princess Emma. It's Mommy, but I know you already knew that. It is so good to finally be able to hold you, my little love.* And she lay on my chest as I kangarooed her for the next two hours. Danny was sitting next to me watching as I loved on her so hard tears ran down my face. It was a perfect moment. The three of us, feeling incredibly grateful for this beautiful moment.

The days, weeks, and months kept passing by. Every day was filled with a new event. Emma was finally growing. The more she grew, the closer we felt to bringing her home. But no matter how much she grew in size, we wouldn't be able to bring her home unless she was able to get extubated (off the breathing machine). By mid-August, the discussion around a tracheostomy was had. We hoped we didn't have to get to that point—we didn't want to put our baby through any more pain. But she couldn't stay intubated for much longer; it was damaging her lungs.

In late August, after an incredibly trying time of meds, infections, PICC lines, resuscitations, and trying every different way to get Emma extubated, we finally did it. After almost four months of being intubated, Emma was finally able to breathe without the tube down her throat and could transition to a nasal cannula for oxygen support. This meant I could now hold my baby any time I wanted without having to be extra careful with the breathing machine attached to her, holding us back from extra love and cuddles. Now we only needed to get Emma to feed enough without the assistance of an NG tube, which was going to be incredibly difficult. By mid-September, we had been in the NICU for 135 days, Emma was six pounds, and she was nowhere near being able to feed on her own. This was when the talk of placing a gastrostomy tube was introduced to us. If Emma couldn't get to a place where she could nourish orally, the only way we would be able to get her home would be with a feeding tube. As hard as it was to make the decision to put our baby through yet another surgery, by the end of September, with no improvement, it was decided Emma needed to come home. Maybe, once she was home, she would thrive better. So, we scheduled a gastrostomy placement for October 4th.

The surgery was a success, and as hard as it was to make that decision, this meant our baby was one step closer to coming home. The hospital made all the necessary arrangements and trained Danny and me how to care for our baby as she was coming home with oxygen, a feeding tube, an apnea monitor, a list of about twenty daily meds, and diagnoses of Bronchopulmonary dysplasia (BPD), anemia of prematurity, and failure to thrive.

Emma had a long road ahead, but we were confident that at home she would be well taken care of, and we could get her to thrive. One day at a time. Before coming home, we were asked to spend the night at the hospital, just one night, for training purposes. The nurses watched as we did their job, the job we would be doing on our own once we were home, to make sure we were as prepared as possible for the journey ahead. They watched and were there for support and any and all questions we had, which were many. We were a nervous wreck and dreaded having to do it all without the assistance of the people who had become a part of our daily lives, our tribe, our support. It was an exhausting night to say the least, but it prepared us somewhat for what was to come. We were ready.

On October 10, 2012, after one of the most trying times in our life, exactly 160 days after giving birth, Danny and I were finally able to bring our baby home. Our doctors, respiratory therapists, and nurses (even the ones who had the day off), Auntie Susan, and Auntie Ashley came to see us off and say goodbye. My mother, my biggest supporter, the one who sat by me day in and day out, was there to help me yet again. We dressed Emma in a beautiful seafoam-colored outfit my mom had especially crocheted for the occasion. I was put in a wheelchair as all new mothers are and was wheeled out as a proud new mother, with Emma in my arms. Danny, my mom, and Emma's medical team were all by my side. Danny's dad pulled up our car and waited for us as we walked out. It was the most incredible moment. And although we weren't walking out of the hospital with a perfectly healthy baby, she was just perfect for us.

Welcome home, baby girl

*Emma was a fighter. I could see her will to learn,
she just needed extra help.*

Life after we left the NICU had some of the hardest moments for Danny and me as parents. There were no more nurses to go to when we felt scared, when the alarms went off, or when we needed a break. Once home, we were all on our own. There was so much to do, to learn, and to process. Yes, Emma had finally come home from the hospital, but we brought home with us not only our daughter but a mini hospital, too.

We set up Emma's nursery with all the equipment: oxygen tank, a huge one that looked like one of those helium tanks you see at Party City; a kangaroo feeding pump the hospital had ordered for us; an apnea monitor, in case, God forbid, she stopped breathing; a pulse oximeter, to be able to watch her heart rate and oxygenation at all times; medication charts, for the 15+ medications she was on; and a camera, to ease our minds.

The plan was to have Emma sleep in her bedroom because that's where her equipment was set up, but the first few nights, we couldn't do it. We were not only scared to leave her alone, but we needed Emma as close to us as possible. So, we set up a temporary space in our tiny bedroom with a portable bassinet we had purchased months prior, and all the equipment she needed. Danny and I took turns getting up to check on her, to set up her feeds and give her medications. This worked the first week, but we were getting run down. After the first week of no sleep, we were barely functioning. The alarms went off every few minutes making it impossible for either of us to sleep. We were exhausted. It wasn't working.

The following week, we decided to try something else. We put Emma back in her room and took shifts staying in there with her, four hours each. Danny took the first shift, 11:00 pm to 3:00 am and I, the second shift, 3:00 am to 7:00 am. We thought this would give us both a few continuous hours of sleep, but that didn't work either. We weren't getting much sleep and neither was Emma. Between messing with her every two hours to change her diaper, give her meds, plug her into the feeding machine, change her clothes after she projectile threw up every night due to her GERD, and re-tape her oxygen nasal cannula because she kept pulling it off, we were all just exhausted. This went on for over two months, and because Emma had to be quarantined and in the most sterile environment due to her weak immune system, we couldn't have people over to help us. Any and all visitors we did have, including our parents, had to be vaccinated with a flu shot, and a Tdap vaccine, otherwise they could not be anywhere near, Emma.

After almost three months of sleepless nights, by the grace of God and the incredible social worker we worked with in the NICU, we were finally going to get some help. Through the hospital, we were connected to a home health service that would send out a re-spite nurse for eight hours a day to help with Emma and give us some relief. We went through an interview process and interviewed quite a few nurses until we found one we were comfortable with. We had the option of choosing the schedule for her, and you best believe we gave her the night shift. She came in at 11:00 pm and left at 7:00 am Monday through Friday. The first few weeks were tough having to get used to having someone in our home and trusting her with our daughter. We still couldn't sleep much. If it wasn't me, it was Danny checking the camera every hour. But day by day, we learned to let go a little and trusted the process. Having a night nurse was giving us some sleep, finally, and also, the opportunity to function so we could better care for our daughter during the day. It was a blessing!

Medical machines, medications, spit-ups, and long-exhaust-ing days was my life for the next two-plus years. If I wanted to go somewhere, I caried a portable oxygen tank, apnea monitor, and portable feeding syringes everywhere I went. I kept them either in the car if I was driving or in the stroller if I ever took her out, which was seldom, especially after a sour experience I'd had on one of my outings. One day, I decided to take Emma with me to shop for a dress for a wedding we had coming up. "Just go babe," Danny encouraged me as I hesitated. "Nothing is going to happen; you'll be fine." I took his advice and loaded Emma in the car along with a stroller and all her machines.

I had just walked into the mall and was about to walk into a store when Emma's machines started to go off, this happened frequently so I wasn't too concerned. I quickly stopped, looked at the pulse oximeter, quieted the alarm and kept walking. The alarm went off again, and this time I was already in the store. People started staring, but I kept doing me. Again, I looked at the pulse oximeter, and when everything looked ok, quieted the machine. When the machine went off again, a lady screamed at me, "What are you doing with that baby, shopping? Shouldn't you be in a hospital? What a selfish mother!" I was embarrassed and felt shame, then guilt. *What am I doing shopping? I'm a terrible mother!* and I ran out of there, tears running down my face. I cried the entire way home. I had been mom-shamed, and any other time I would have said something back. I would have said, "My baby is perfectly fine, maybe next time instead of screaming at a complete stranger, you can ask if we are ok!" but I was already so vulnerable that it instantly hurt and shamed me. Needless to say, I didn't go shopping at the mall again for a long time.

I stayed home a lot around this time, unless it was absolutely necessary for me to go out. Not only was it time consuming and exhausting for me to carry a baby and her medical equipment everywhere I went, but it was mentally stressful. I obviously knew how to care for my daughter and had a handle on things, but the stares, hushed comments, and the judgement from others made it very difficult for me to want to be out in public on my own. Once in a while when Danny got off work early during the week, or on the weekends, we'd take Emma on walks to the beach to get some fresh air and watch the sunset. We'd set up a family picnic and let her roll around and play. She always loved that. This might be the reason she loves watching the sunset so much now, too.

Emma started receiving therapy services through the regional center to help with her development soon after coming home from the NICU. She received occupational therapy, early intervention therapy, oral therapy, physical therapy, and speech therapy. They each came to our home once a week for an hour, sat on Emma's pink rug in her room, and taught her new skills every day through play. I sat in on every session, trying to soak up all the information I could so that when the therapists weren't around, I too, could continue to teach Emma and help her thrive. I took notes, asked questions, and learned skills I never thought I needed. I used to think kids just knew what to do. Development was a process that naturally happened without having to teach it. But our case was not like that. Emma had to learn to do the basic skills she naturally didn't develop. And my one and only goal was to get my daughter thriving.

It was a lengthy process, to say the least, but one day at a time we started seeing progress. Emma went from a limp, weak baby, to a stronger one every day. Suddenly, she could sit up on her own. She reached for things. She was a little more coordinated. Because of her limitations with wires and her feeding tube, Emma was never able to do tummy time, and she never crawled, even though we worked extensively to get her to. But eventually, she was starting to scoot around on her bottom the way most infants do. Emma was a fighter; I could see her will to learn, she just needed extra help.

There were days she got frustrated and wanted nothing to do with her therapists, and though she wasn't vocal she got her point across. Her personality definitely came through. "Ok, Emma," her therapist would say as Emma threw toys at her, "I see you're not in the mood today." But more often than not, Emma was willing to learn. When she didn't speak for a long time, we found other ways to teach her to communicate. Emma's first language was actually sign language. I had taken some ASL classes in college and figured, why not? Together with her occupational therapist, we taught her to sign. My baby was working hard, and we were starting to see results. Once upon a time, while in NICU, they told us Emma would be developmentally delayed. They didn't know how extensive, but she would need assistance for a long time. I didn't want to believe this, and as long as I had a say, I would do everything in my power to change that outcome.

Although it took her a little extra time, my daughter eventually learned to talk. Dadda was her first word. Mamma came soon after. It was music to our ears. She babbled and babbled until she could form full sentences. Once we were able to desensitize her hands and the bottom of her feet, she started to walk. First, with the assistance of a walker, and eventually, all on her own. That was her shining moment; she even clapped for herself as we clapped for her. There was no stopping her now. And we were enjoying every moment, every step of the way. The things most people took for granted, we had to work extra hard to achieve, but we were headed in the right direction.

I will never forget the day Emma ate her first food by mouth. We had been working with Emma's oral therapist for over a year, stimulating and desensitizing Emma's mouth, and one day it happened. I made Emma's favorite, sweet potato puree, and though it took her thirty minutes, she ate the entire thing: a whole tablespoon of Mommy's homemade sweet potato puree. We celebrated that day unlike any other; our baby ate real food! I have never looked at a tablespoon or sweet potato the same again.

Emma eventually transferred from in-home services to in-center therapies, and this was when she started thriving even more. Maybe it was because she saw other children or because it was a different atmosphere with more to see and people to play with or a combination of it all, but slowly she was meeting her goals. She loved going to Napa Center for physical therapy because they had a giant obstacle course and she had more freedom to "play." Her speech therapist always had a surprise for her, too. And at Brite Kids, she got to see her favorite OT, Marlyna. *"All done OT, all done OT, all done OT; we'll see you next week,"* she'd sing the entire way home. Developmentally, our baby was thriving and happy!

Healthwise, Emma struggled a lot. Not long after coming home from the NICU, she was back at the hospital time and time again—at least once a month. One of these times almost cost us her life. Most other hospital stays were due to her underdeveloped lungs and chronic lung disease. Emma was very susceptible to infection, and other people's germs and colds. Emma could catch a slight cold and it would instantly turn into pneumonia, and to the hospital we would go. Every stay was usually a week long. We spent sleepless nights in hospital rooms soothing her to sleep, telling her it was almost over. "You have to be strong and fight this, little love," was all we could say, over and over until she'd fall asleep with tears in her eyes. It was so hard on her; she struggled so much to breathe and usually needed extra oxygen. It was hard on us to see her suffer so much and cry in pain. Her veins hadn't even regenerated from the NICU before she was already being poked and prodded again. We dreaded IVs and usually had to get one of her NICU nurses to start one because they were already familiar with her blown, tiny veins. The hospital already knew us and Emma's long medical chart, so that helped, but with every stay my baby suffered again and again.

Eventually, in due time, we weaned Emma off the medical machines one by one. First, it was her oxygen; our baby was finally able to breathe without oxygen assistance. Our healing prayers were being answered. Then, after a few sleep studies with great numbers, her doctors removed her apnea monitor. And three years after it was placed, twice, her feeding tube was removed. We worked so hard to get our baby to eat on her own and it finally happened. She was thriving. The pulse oximeter we kept for a long time because we were too scared to not see Emma's heart and oxygenation numbers constantly, but eventually, our baby was cordless, and we could hold and play with her like any other child!

★★★

I wish I could say Emma is fully healed today, but sadly, that is not the case. She's had to undergo a few more surgeries after blown out ear drums and feeding tube issues. She's had many more hospital stays due to her lung disease and breathing struggles. She's had sleep study after sleep study to try and figure out why she stops breathing throughout the night. She's had many procedures to try and heal her intestinal issues and to figure out why her vocal cords are so damaged. She's had an insane number of tests, shots, and labs to get her to thrive and grow. And we, as well as her cardiologist, have to keep a very close eye on her heart, as it has scared us a few times.

Emma continues to see a speech pathologist that helps with her vocal cord trauma (from intubation) and teaches her techniques on how to properly breathe, because even that is something she continues to learn how to do. Currently, she sees cardiology, pulmonary, gastroenterology, endocrinology, and genetics doctors as well as a primary doctor monthly to get her to thrive and grow the way she is meant to. I have spent sleepless nights at my daughter's bedside, worrying as she fights to breathe. I have watched her spike fevers that have turned her limp and lethargic. I wake up most nights to check in on her while she sleeps, just to make sure she hasn't forgotten to breathe.

Life as a micro-preemie doesn't end the day you walk out of the NICU doors. Life as a micro-preemie parent is never-ending.

Faby Ryan

Still, us

To not growing old and grumpy!

As stressful as our life was with Emma's health, diagnoses, hospital visits, and overall parenthood, Danny and I always found a way to connect with each other, to make time at the end of the day and not lose one another. Because some days, it felt like we were living two separate lives. His life mostly at work and mine at home, caring for Emma.

Being a stay-at-home mom was a job that easily consumed me. It was hard for me to think about anything but Emma, the house, the responsibilities, and everything else in between. But Danny was great at reminding me that *we* still mattered. Our *marriage* was important, too. And that we *should* always make time for *us*. "What happens the day Emma grows up, decides to build a life of her own, and moves away?" he said. "We will still have each other, but only if we keep building and nurturing our marriage." He was right—I knew he was right, but I'd get so overwhelmed and frustrated being stuck at home and not having a life, a social life outside of my bubble, that I didn't want to hear it sometimes.

"You stay with Emma then. I'll go back to work," I'd say.

Over time, I came around, but only after I requested a night off. One day, after an incredibly hard day at home, I snapped. Danny walked in the house to a crazy, overwhelmed, crying mess of a woman. "I need a day off," I said in between tears. "Once a week I need you to come home early so I can leave. Don't ask me where I am going or what I am doing; I am just leaving!"

Danny looked at me confused, "Ok," he said, "if it will help *this,*" he said as he twirled his pointed finger at me.

"Well, it will. I want every Wednesday off!" Why Wednesday? I figured it was the middle of the week and it would break up my days. *No more crazy-falling-apart wife.* Once I calmed down, I explained to Danny I was feeling incredibly overwhelmed. "I need to feel like a person again," I said, and he agreed. So, on Wednesdays, Danny came home from work early, 4:00 pm, and took care of

Emma all on his own. And I had a few hours to myself. Sometimes all I did was park at the end of the street in an empty parking lot and listened to music on the radio, other times I'd call a friend and catch up, but it was my time. And it made me a better wife and mother for it.

Eventually, we had a rhythm going. A few times a week, at the end of the day, once the nurse showed up and we knew Emma was taken care of, we'd go out back, have a glass of wine, and catch up on our day and talk about *us*. Other days, we'd snuggle in bed and watch our favorite TV shows, either *The Voice* or *Chopped*, until we fell asleep. Once in a while if we felt comfortable, we'd go out to a late dinner at our favorite restaurant, Gyu-Kaku Japanese BBQ, for their late happy hour menu. Our life was filled with the chaos of work, parenthood, and the occasional meltdown, but all in all Danny and I made a great team. We knew which battles to pick and when to throw in the towel. Above all, our marriage was just as important as our parent life and our daughter was. And that always kept us going.

For six incredible years, Danny and I made our marriage a priority. Not always or daily because we had plenty of bad moments and unhappy days like any other couple, but we always envisioned and talked about the old, wrinkly couple we wanted to be at the end of this marriage. Every time we celebrated an anniversary and made a toast, Danny always ended it with "To not growing old and grumpy!" That became his signature toast. We randomly talked about what we'd do with our lives as we got old and retired.

"Where do you want to retire?" Danny asked.

"San Diego," I said. San Diego always seemed a perfect spot for me.

"How many grandchildren do you think Emma is going to give us?" he continued.

"Lots, I hope ten at least; I want to be a super cool grandma to ten," I said, and he laughed. We had so many plans for a future.

Anniversary

Cheers, to the next 50!
Because marrying you was the smartest thing I ever did.

On Saturday October 3, 2015, Danny and I celebrated our 6th year wedding anniversary. "Can you believe we made it to six years!?" I asked.

"I can," Danny said. "You can't get rid of me, you'd have to kill me first. 'Til death do us part, remember?" Six years. It seemed so long ago that we'd gotten married, and like yesterday all at the same time. Our lives had gotten so busy and so consumed with all of Emma's therapies, medical needs, surgeries, and hospitalizations that sometimes our marriage got put on the back burner, not intentionally, but routinely.

"Ok, my love," Danny said to me excitedly Thursday night, "I have made plans for our anniversary Saturday; it's a surprise. I booked a sitter (grandparents), and we will drop her off tomorrow night, so we can enjoy a full day to ourselves. All you have to do is be ready by 10 am Saturday; wear something casual." I was excited. I loved Danny's surprises. He knew how much it meant to me when people put thought, time, and effort into making someone else's day special, and this was definitely one of those special days for me.

Friday morning, Danny woke me up with sloppy kisses (not just from him, but from Emma too), hugs, and an immense amount of love! This was our mini family pre-anniversary celebration since we would be dropping Emma off at my mom's later in the day and were not going to see her on our actual anniversary day. Together, he and Emma handed me the most beautiful bouquet of white roses (one of our favorite flowers), a beautifully wrapped present, and a card. Danny knew how much I loved hand-written cards. I've kept and treasured every card he ever gave me, the card read:

Once upon a time…
I promised to love you forever-
to stay by your side through good times and bad.

It was the biggest promise I ever made.
Yet each year, as forever draws closer
I'm struck by how simple it has been...
because marrying you was the smartest thing I ever did.
Happy Anniversary
He then added:
My life has been made complete with you
& our little monkey in it. I am truly blessed to have you
as my wife. You are a great wife & mother.
Love you the most,
Your Hubby

I was in tears by the end of the card. There was no greater gift to me than his written expressions of love, words he wrote in solitude, at his most vulnerable, straight from the heart. I don't think Danny knew this, but he was a beautiful writer. He had a way with words that not many have. His love and attention to detail and the effort he put into everything he did was just beautiful to witness and be a part of. Those sentiments are my most prized Danny possessions.

Later that night, we went and dropped Emma off at my parent's house, Emma was excited to see Nana and vice versa. We were excited to spend some time together, alone, something that didn't happen often. We left my parent's house eager to start the anniversary celebrations. Upon getting home, we went out to the backyard, Danny started a cozy fire in the firepit, and we opened a bottle of red wine and relaxed for the rest of the evening. By 10 am the next morning, anniversary day, I was dressed and ready to go. Danny said casual, so I wore jean shorts and a flowy off-the-shoulder colorful top—casual, but still cute.

When I walked outside, our ride awaited us: two beach cruisers. We started the morning with a seven-mile bike ride on the trail behind our house to Seal Beach. What a fun way to start our day. We pedaled with the sun kissing our faces as we chatted the entire time.

"Where are we going?" I kept asking Danny.

"You'll see soon enough," he said. I loved the suspense and excitement in his voice as he tried to surprise me. The trail was long, so once in a while we would stop to take a drink of water and stand by the waterway in awe of the flying fish. Then we'd get back on the bikes and race each other on and off the rest of the way. Danny was a pro bike rider and a lot better than I was. As a child, he raced BMX bikes and was also a very good dirt bike rider. I, on the other hand, was a scaredy-cat on a bike. I had a terrible experience as a little girl; I got hit by a car while riding a bike and that had left some trauma. I had a hard time with shaking, and it usually took a while for me to ease into the bike idea. Danny knew this. In fact, the cute little pink beach cruiser I was riding, Danny had gifted to me our first Christmas together after I told him my story and mentioned I hadn't ridden a bike in years. "I am going to help you get over this fear," he'd said. He was determined and promised to always watch over me. He never broke his promise.

It took us a couple hours (with all the stopping) to get to our destination, Schooner or Later, a really cool brunch place at the Long Beach Marina I had been wanting try for a while. One of my old bosses raved about it for years and I'd never had the opportunity to go. The place was known for its amazing brunch menu and killer mimosas. The only bummer was they got crazy crowded all the time and they took no reservations; it was first come, first served. Our wait time was about an hour, but this time we didn't care for a change because we were flying solo, no baby! We ordered a bottle of champagne while we waited and then sat on a little bench overlooking the marina as we replayed some of our best moments over the last six years. And as much as we wanted to be grown-ups and avoid baby talk, Emma was a huge topic of conversation.

We discussed how proud we were of her and how far she'd come. We toasted and embraced each other as we talked about our plans for the near future in regard to work and some travel we wanted to squeeze in that year. We also discussed the idea of another baby. It was something that had been in our thoughts for a while; we had even discussed the idea with my OB-GYN, who was also a fertility specialist. My doctor had given us the go ahead and even gave me a prescription for medication I would have to get on when we were ready to start trying. We were incredibly scared given everything we'd been through in the baby department, but we were hopeful a healthy baby could be in our future. We really wanted to give Emma a sibling, maybe the little brother we always imagined she'd have.

We had one of the most intimate conversations over that hour, which could have been filled with irritation from having to wait so long, but instead we really took the moment in. It was a beautiful early fall day. The sun was shining and our love was flowing. We even managed to do a little lovey photo sesh right before they called us letting us know our table was ready. We ordered some yummy food and toasted some more as we ate and chatted away. It was the perfect anniversary date, except for the fact that by the end of the brunch we were a little tipsy and still had to ride our bikes back home, against the wind. We laughed the entire ride home, huffing and puffing as we pedaled away, and more in love and filled with happy endorphins than we had been in a long time. By the time we got home and put the bikes away, we were exhausted.

"The day isn't over yet, but wanna take a little nap?" Danny suggested.

"Sure!" Our goal was to nap, but we did very little of that.

A couple of hours later, we got up, showered, and got dressed for our next event of the day. Danny made reservations at a nearby spa in Long Beach for a couple's massage. Danny was not the spa/massage type; to him, it was very intimidating laying naked and getting rubbed by a stranger, but he knew how much I loved massages. I thought it was very romantic. I loved how open Danny always was to doing things out of his comfort zone. Plus, he just loved me and wanted to make me happy. Walking in, the place was a little creepy looking; it was incredibly dark and decorated with red velvet furniture and lots of gold figurines everywhere. It did not look like the traditional Burke Williams open space spas we had been to before. We looked at each other and shrugged our shoulders. *What the hell,* we thought, and followed in. Despite how creepy the place was and how crappy the massages were, Danny and I walked out of there laughing and happy as clams. We were spending an incredible intimate time together, something we had needed for a long time.

After the massage, we again headed home to wash up and got dressed for dinner. I love dinners, especially the romantic kind where I get to dress up and feel like a woman, something I don't get in my everyday workout clothes and bun (but without the workout). For dinner, I wore a sexy little black dress that sat right above the knee. With no baby to look after, I didn't have to worry about bending over and showing more than I intended. Danny wore his staple blue button up shirt, his black slacks, and black dress shoes. He looked really handsome. I loved seeing him dressed up for me. Still not knowing where we were headed—another one of Danny's surprises—we continued with our evening. On the car ride there, we did what we knew best: Karaoke to our favorite duets. Our favorite was "Need You Now" by Lady Antebellum.

This was our go-to at every karaoke bar. Danny would belt it out with so much emotion his singing skills didn't matter. It was always a great time. And Karaoke in the car was how we practiced our skills. We finally arrived and ended our night at Maggiano's Little Italy in Los Angeles, one of our favorite Italian restaurants. The ambiance there was always on point: classy yet casual, not too over the top where you felt like you had to whisper to each other in order to not disturb other patrons. Danny and I were not in a shushed mood that day; we were silly and laughed more than we could remember doing in a long time.

Similar to how we'd done on our official first date, we ordered a bottle of red wine and some of our favorite dishes to share: seafood linguini for me and for him, his favorite, chicken piccata, extra capers. The restaurant brought us a yummy chocolate dessert to celebrate our evening, which we quickly devoured, and we made one last toast *to us*. The evening had been a perfect one full of laughs, fun surprises, and contrary to what Danny thought, it was incredibly romantic. My knight in shining crutches had given me just what my heart needed on such a beautiful milestone for us. After dinner, we headed home, put some country music on the TV music channel, and danced the night away.

"Happy six-year wedding anniversary babe; I love you."

"I love you, too!"

"Cheers, to the next fifty."

"Cheers, to not growing old and grumpy!"

1. My 26th birthday was spent riding the Harley along the coast and to the cliffs of Palos Verdes, Ca. 2. One of the many SpaceX (epic) parties we got to attend. 3. This was the first super-date I ever won; A gondola sunset cruise along the Newport Beach Harbor. 4. January 9, 2009, one of the only photos I have of our secret marriage; Nothing fancy, but just perfect! 5. This is one of my favorite engagement photos, shot in the streets of Santa Monica. 6. When time stood still... 7. October 3, 2009- the never-ending walk down the aisle toward the love of my life, on our wedding day. 8. The beginning of our happily ever after... 9. Baby-mooning in San Francisco three days before Emma was born, never imagining what was ahead.

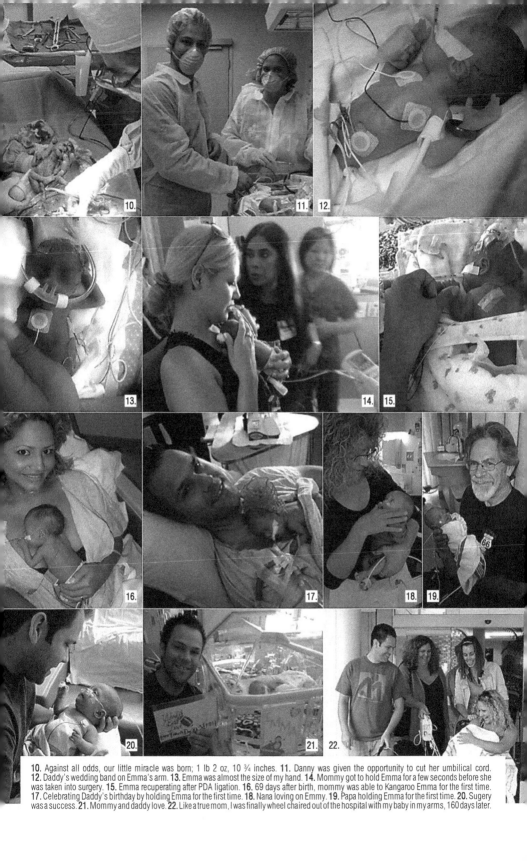

10. Against all odds, our little miracle was born; 1 lb 2 oz, 10 ¾ inches. **11.** Danny was given the opportunity to cut her umbilical cord. **12.** Daddy's wedding band on Emma's arm. **13.** Emma was almost the size of my hand. **14.** Mommy got to hold Emma for a few seconds before she was taken into surgery. **15.** Emma recuperating after PDA ligation. **16.** 69 days after birth, mommy was able to Kangaroo Emma for the first time. **17.** Celebrating Daddy's birthday by holding Emma for the first time. **18.** Nana loving on Emmy. **19.** Papa holding Emma for the first time. **20.** Sugery was a success. **21.** Mommy and daddy love. **22.** Like a true mom, I was finally wheel chaired out of the hospital with my baby in my arms, 160 days later.

23. Emma's firs time seeing the outside world. **24.** Our first family picnic at the beach to watch the sunset. **25.** My little miracle survived yet another major surgery. **26.** Our holidays were spent between Emma's hospital room and The Ronald Mc Donald house across the street from the hospital. **27.** Emma's personality was starting to show. **28.** We were finally home, again. **29.** Mami Celia and Emma. **30.** Our poor baby couldn't catch a break. **31.** Danny trying to distract us and help us pass the time in the hospital.

32. Emma's Baptism. 33. Emma's graduation from Brite Kids, early intervention. 34. We got the keys to our new house, still our current home. 35. On every river trip I always made sure to snap a photo of Danny and Emma living their best lives! 36. Emma's first day of school, Buffum total learning center. 37. Visits with Grandma Vi (Grams). 38. My two favorite people in the world. 39. The gorge was Danny's favorite place at the river. 40. The day before we headed home after the accident we had an intimate memorial at the river, this was the place where I last held my husband. 41. "Why is dadda so old?" Emma asked. "Will you get old and die too, mommy?" My daughter's biggest fear is me getting old and dying like daddy. 42. Our first family photos without Danny, two monarchs stuck together one on top of the other joined our shoot.

43. Papa had this plaque made, which we put under the needles bridge in Danny's memory. **44.** My memorial tattoo with Danny's last anniversary card writings to me, his penmanship and all. **45.** Green Hills cemetery. **46. – 47.** Emma's fifth Birthday; Cinco de Mayo fiesta! **#ShowingEmmyTheWorld: 48. – 49.** Disneyworld. **50.** Cabo San Lucas, Mexico Airport. **51.** Cabo San Lucas, Mexico. **52.** Greece. **53.** Florida. **54.** Colorado.

#ShowingEmmyTheWorld: **55.** Havasupai. **56.** Costa Rica. **57.** Penninsula Papapagayo, Costa Rica. **58.** Disneyworld. **59.** Chicago. **60.** Havasupai. **61.** Mammoth Lakes, Ca. **62.** Sonoma, Ca. **63.** San Francsco, Ca.

A Time to Live

This place was sacred to us.
So sacred that without him, I could not see myself in this place gain.

Thursday, October 8, 2015

"Babe, why don't we leave for the river house tonight instead of tomorrow? Traffic on Fridays is terrible. We can go slow to see how the Jeep runs, and you can follow behind with Emmy?!" Danny suggested.

"Umm, ok. I am already pretty much packed; we can make it work!" I replied. I was always up for anything, especially when it came to us going on yet another adventure with our little family. We were meeting our friends that were already staying at our river house, and we wanted to take advantage of the weekend as much we could. This would be our last river trip of the season before the weather got too cold to be out on the water. We figured Emmy could sleep on the way and be rested by morning. Danny had just purchased a Jeep that we would be leaving at the river house to launch the boat in and out of the water when we went. So for this trip, we were driving two cars out, and coming home together in one. I followed behind him to make sure everything with the new vehicle was running ok, or in case something did break, and he needed my help, I was right behind. The drive out to the river house at night is long and very dark: four hours through the desert. The house is located where California, Nevada, and Arizona meet, in between Laughlin, Nevada, and Lake Havasu, Arizona.

We loaded up the car with just the essentials for us: clothes, food, and drinks, and everything else was what Emma would need: meds, food, favorite toys, and a new life jacket we'd just purchased for her that she was super excited for. This would be the first time she would be able to go swimming without her feeding tube, a day we'd prayed for so long. When we purchased the river house, we completely set it up with everything we thought we could possibly need so we didn't have to drag things back and forth every time we went. It was the best thing we could have done. Not having to bring too much stuff sure helped, especially with having Emma. The amount of stuff one needs when traveling with kids is beyond me. We got all our things together and put the peanut in the car. With no time wasted, we were on the road. Danny and I texted each other randomly throughout the drive just to make sure we were both ok, even though I was right behind him.

9:20 pm

Me: Do you wanna just drive straight?

Danny: No. Stop at Barstow.

12:34 am

Me: 55?

Danny: Running low on gas.

Me: Wanna pull over and fill? I'm so tired now. My eyes are sleepy.

Danny: No place 2. We will make it. Just can't waste. Me too. I'm thirsty though.

Me: I can still do a glass of wine though.

We pulled into Colorado Shores and then into our driveway around 1:00 am. The house was dark, and the friends that were at the house already were asleep in the guest bedroom upstairs. We brought Emma upstairs and into her bedroom next door; she was sound asleep. We headed back downstairs and unloaded the car quietly so we didn't wake anyone up. Once we were done unloading and putting things away, we went into the kitchen downstairs and opened up a bottle of red wine, a Josh Cabernet Sauvignon to be exact, our favorite. We walked out back to the bottom deck of the house where the still, cool October night air and the glimmering moon reflecting on the lagoon were waiting for us. The lagoon was our favorite space at the house and was one of the main reasons we purchased this place. The energy and peacefulness that is felt when you sit there looking out and listening to the water flowing is breathtaking—at least for us it was. We were water lovers, and this was the perfect place for us.

I can still remember the weekend we drove out to Lake Havasu to shop for a potential river home. Emma was still very little and required lots of medical attention, equipment, and support. Before this, we had made an attempt at a river trip with friends; we'd been locked down for so long, and we just wanted to feel normal.

We had booked and stayed at a hotel room only to run home that same night at about 3 am. We'd set up Emma's sleeping arrangements next to us on the floor because she had to be attached to her oxygen tank, feeding machine, apnea monitor, and pulse oximeter. Every two hours, one of us had to get up, stop the feeding machine, clean it out in the bathroom sink, and set it up for the next feed an hour later. Needless to say, it had been impossible and there was no resting or getting any sleep. So, we grabbed our stuff, put Emma in the car, and drove home. Bummed and disappointed that as much as we had tried to have a normal weekend out with friends, in our situation, it was just unrealistic.

After that weekend, the idea of purchasing a place out at the river was on our minds. If we wanted to start living life a little and getting out once in a while to breathe fresh air and have a little fun, we couldn't possibly do it out of a hotel room, not with Emma's medical situation. "What if we buy a house at the river?" Danny had asked.

"A house? You really think we will be coming to the river that often?" I replied.

"I hope so! And maybe if we had a place of our own, it would make life a little easier for us. If you or Emma weren't up for going out on the water for whatever reason, you would at least have a comfortable place to be in, a place of our own." That made so much sense and we really wanted to start living a little. The river was a close but far enough away place so that it definitely felt like a mini-vacation.

"Ok," I said, "let's do it. Let's start looking!" I didn't have to tell Danny "Let's start looking" for something because he was already online doing his research.

Redfin became his best friend. And when I least expected, he already had pages of listings printed out that he wanted us to go see. We picked out a weekend, scheduled a realtor, and went out on the hunt for our little adventure home. The trip wasn't as easy or as fun as we thought it would it be. The listings we had to view were horrible in person, way overpriced, too far from the lake, and just not what we'd had in mind. That day at dinner, after considering all of our options, Danny and I decided that although the idea was great, this probably was not the best time for us to buy a river house. We were a little disappointed, as we'd just wanted to add a little normalcy and fun to our lives while also being mindful of our daughter and her medical condition.

The next morning on our way home, Danny pulled out one last printed listing he hadn't showed me because it was on another part of the river, not in Lake Havasu. "It's on the way out," he said. "Wanna go look at it?"

"Sure, but we're just gonna look at it from the outside. We don't have a realtor anymore, remember?! And we said no house for now."

"I know," Danny said. So, on our way home, we stopped to look at this one last house. The listing didn't give much detail on the home, so we didn't know what to expect. We pulled up to the front and we were immediately intrigued. The house was in a private little community next to a golf course and a short two-minute walk to the riverfront. We got out of the car and walked around the property, only to find the backyard had an actual lagoon.

"What?! There's a lagoon? And so much space back there!" I said to Danny.

Danny looked at me with interested eyes and blurted out, "I really wanna see the inside!"

"Me too!"

"What if we call the realtor on the seller sign and see if she'd be willing to open the house up for us?" We dialed the number on the Keller Williams sign and got a hold of a lady. We told her we were standing outside the house and were really interested in looking at it.

"I can be there in twenty minutes," she said.

"I thought we were done with houses for now," I said to Danny.

"We are," he said, "we are just looking at it." The realtor was at the house in no time. We were anxious to see the inside but also trying to stay realistic. Upon opening the door and walking into the foyer, we just knew.

The lady walked in and started chatting away. When she wasn't looking, Danny and I stared at each other and mouthed, *OH MY GOD!* The lady looked back at us to see what we thought, but we played it off and just nodded. "It's nice." Every time the lady looked away, we stared at each other, mouthed something, and laughed. We loved the house. It needed some work, of course, but all in all, it was the best house we had seen all weekend. The realtor locked up the house, gave us a card, and told us if we needed anything to give her a call. We walked out of that house in a river home dream.

"What do we do now?" I asked.

"I really like the house," Danny said. "What do you think?!"

"I like it too, of course I do, but what about the plan?" The plan was out the window, and we both knew this.

"I think we should talk to a realtor and put an offer in," Danny stated. We jumped in the car and on our way home called our broker, Nancy.

"Hi Nancy, there's this house at the river—we want to buy it!" Less than a week later, we put an offer on the house. And by December 2013, the house was ours. We threw a housewarming/New Year's Eve party a couple weeks later to inaugurate our little family vacation home, The Ryan River House. My family gladly made the trip! It was the perfect house to start living our best life in. We made such incredible memories that I will forever carry in my heart.

And now, here I was with my husband two years later, enjoying a yummy glass of wine as we got ready to enjoy a beautiful weekend. We walked over and sat on the teak lounge chairs across from the firepit on the bottom deck overlooking the water, and we made a toast: "To our last river trip of the season, and to making it home safe." I had been a little nervous toward the end of our drive there; the Jeep had been running low on gas and we were a little scared of not making it to the house safely.

"Cheers, my love, to making it here safe and to a great weekend ahead!"

"Cheers, babe!"

We sat for a while, staring out and contemplating the beautiful night. It was a little chilly so Danny held me close and cuddled me a little extra. We made plans for the following day: "Let's try and get up early. We can enjoy the day as long as possible." Danny was an extra early riser when we came to the river; the earlier the better. I, on the other hand, loved my sleep here.

"I am on vacation," I'd argue.

"Ok, let's get up, have a light breakfast, and try and head out by 8 am." Danny would say.

"Fine! Can we just enjoy now and not talk about waking up

early? We haven't even gone to bed to wake up yet!" I could be such a baby at times, but Danny was good at compromising with me, even when he'd roll his eyes and get irritated.

"Oh, did I tell you Tim from SpaceX might come join us tomorrow?" Danny said.

"Tim?" I asked.

"Yeah, he's friends with Daniel and Elizabeth from the NICU, remember?"

"Oh, yeah, that's fun, when does he get here?"

"I'm not sure, sometime tomorrow. He said he would call me. He'll just be joining us for the day.

I'd never met Tim, but I'd heard good things. *It should be a super fun weekend. I'm excited to relax and spend time with my two loves.*

The next conversation we had is one that I still can't shake. One I still can't believe we had. I'm not sure what I was thinking or what brought on such a deep subject, but as I was looking out at the water, embraced in Danny's arms, and feeling so loved and in love, I looked at him and said, "Babe, if something ever happened to you, I don't know that I could ever come back here." Danny looked at me, but remailed silent, probably trying to process what I'd just said and wondering where it was coming from.

After a few moments of silence, he said, "If something ever happened to you, it would be hard, and it would suck, but I hope that I could turn the sadness around and still be able to make beautiful memories here."

"I don't know that I could."

Danny was always the more practical one. He always looked at the big picture, and his outlook on things was always positive. Even when it was hard to look at the bright side, he always tried to. I, on the other hand, have always been more emotional. I take everything to heart, and I carry my heart on my sleeve. This had been a hypothetical conversation, and to this day, I am not sure what prompted it. It was a feeling, an urge to let him know I loved him and this place was sacred to us. So sacred that without him, I could not see myself in it; it would not and could not ever be the same.

We embraced and looked at each other solemnly. "Oh, babe," he said as he kissed my forehead and held me tight. I could feel the cool breeze my face.

"It's getting cold. We should get inside and go to bed," I said. We finished the last sips of wine and walked in the house. We went upstairs and checked in on Emma before heading to our bedroom; she was fast asleep. It was past 2:00 am. We got into bed and called it a night. I couldn't get over the conversation we'd just had. What had made me get so emotional and say those things to him? I tried shaking it off, shaking the thought and the feelings off. *Of course nothing is going happen to him!*

I snuggled and laid on his chest like I always did when I couldn't sleep. The sound of his heart was always soothing to me, and it helped me settle. Danny embraced me in his arms and we went to sleep.

"Good night, my love," I said

"Good night, babe."

Faby Ryan

Fate

If I had known this would be our last day together,
I would have never let you go.

When we docked at the beach that beautiful early October, Friday evening, the warm sun kissing our skin, and the cold water touching our feet, I didn't realize this was the night that would forever change my life. Fall was soon approaching, and we wanted so much to enjoy the last bit of summer at the river. This would be our last trip of the season, and we wanted to make it last as long as we could. Everything was perfect. We had a beautiful day on the water, coasting, and beaching up and down the Gorge, Danny's favorite place. Our friends were with us for the weekend and the weather couldn't have been more perfect, 100 degrees in October, pretty ideal. Our daughter was thriving and having the time of her life; finally, things with her health were getting better. Our family was in a beautiful place. We were with friends and had just met up with another one of Danny's friends to join in on the fun.

"We want to go on a short boys boat run, my love, last of the night. We will be in shortly," Danny said. He handed me Emma, and I kissed him on our way out.

"Come on my little love, let's let Dadda have a little fun! We'll get dinner started. Don't take too long guys, have a fun ride!" I said.

We went up to the house, my girlfriend, Emma, and I (the girls). We put our beach stuff down, and I let Emma play while my girl-friend and I searched our phones for some music to plug into the Bose dock I had sitting on top of the kitchen counter. We were in the middle of getting dinner ready, singing, dancing, chopping, and laughing the night away, still in our bathing suits from the day's river adventure, when my friend got a call from her husband. We figured the boys were calling to let us know they were on their way back home. Because her phone was plugged in on the dock, she answered the call on speaker mode.

We were excited when she answered, "Hurry up guys, are you back yet or what?" We couldn't really hear him, so we made fun and teased him about when they were getting back home. It wasn't until he yelled at her to take him off speaker, *now*, that the seriousness in his voice sunk in. She quickly took the call off speaker and off the Bose dock. All of a sudden, I felt a shift in her body language and in her facial expression. It went from laughter and joy to utter silence and seriousness. She listened to her husband intently while staring at me and trying to avoid my gaze at the same time. I couldn't figure out what was happening or what he was saying to her. Worry started to creep in.

"Are they on their way back? Everything ok?" I asked. She was still on the phone, saying nothing. *"What happened? What's going on? Everything ok—what is happening?"* I repeated. When she hung up the phone and, in a panic, said, "We have to go to the nearest hospital; something happened," my heart just knew. I knew it was Danny. I knew Danny was hurt. I could feel it in my bones. "What do you know? What did your husband say?"

"I don't know," was all she could say. "He just said to go to the nearest hospital!"

"I don't know where the nearest hospital is!" I replied. I quickly put on a white cover-up over my bathing suit and grabbed Emma. My friend threw on some clothes and a black hat and we hurriedly ran downstairs to my car. I put Emma in her car seat, buckled her up, and started to drive. I didn't even know which way we were going or where the nearest hospital was, so we had to look it up on the phone map. We drove in a panic, unsure of what to expect. My friend didn't say much; she was quiet. I had so many questions—ones she couldn't answer.

"What DID he say? Did he tell you anything?" I asked.

"He didn't say much!" That made me panic even more. My brain went there, to that place, you know that place you're not supposed to go to, but your brain does anyway? I played a million different scenarios in my mind. What could have possibly happened between the time they left to now? It hadn't even been an hour! *What if he's badly hurt?* No scenario gave me peace of mind; none of them gave me a good outcome. I have always been a worrier. Danny would always tell me I worried too much, "Relax those brows, babe, you worry too much!"

My heart was racing with fear. *Danny's hurt; I know he is hurt.* As we got close to the main road, out of the golf course area where our house is, we saw a roaring trail of firetrucks and ambulances heading toward us. We stopped the car as we watched the chaos of sirens. I looked around at the surroundings to see if I could get a glimpse of anything. To the right side of the road, under the Needles Bridge behind some tall bushes, I noticed an RV community. I quickly asked my friend if she thought we could get through. She got out of the car to check, but it was full of bushes and was fenced in. When she came back, she had scratches everywhere and was bleeding. "Are you ok?" I asked. She shrugged it off and jumped back in the car.

"Don't go to the hospital," I said to her, "follow those ambulances!" Something told me that if we followed them, I would find Danny. We turned the car around and followed the lights and sirens back toward the golf course. Sure enough, they'd entered the RV resort we had previously tried to get into from the side of the road. The road into this place was long and unpaved; it seemed never-ending, and we didn't know where we were going. We were just following the lights. I had never been under the Needles Bridge area other than driving past it on the boat with Danny.

The further we drove in, the louder the noise got, and the brighter the lights from the firetrucks and ambulances got. After what seemed like forever, we finally came to the end of the road. We pulled over to the right, stopped the car, and parked. I quickly grabbed Emma out of her car seat and we ran out the door. I looked around in every direction trying to find a familiar face, something, anything that would point me the right way. I wasn't familiar with this area of the river. The RV resort was private and only occupants had access to it.

Down a small grass hill, I could see the Needles Bridge, and below it, a private beach, and an immense amount of chaos. It was dusk and starting to get dark. The moon wasn't shining bright in the water as it normally did. The three of us started to walk down the hill, and the more we walked down, the more panic I felt in my heart. The scene was right out of a movie, one of those police scenes where it's hard to know what is what and who is who. When I turned to my left, I saw my friend's husband sitting in the back of an ambulance with his two boys; they looked ok. They were sitting up, talking, seemingly not badly hurt, but it was hard to tell. I'm not sure if he waved us over or not, my mind was frantically searching for Danny, but I couldn't see him. He wasn't with him. My friend quickly ran to her family in relief. I, too, was relieved they were ok, but where was Danny—where was my husband?!

I told my friend to please stay with Emma while I went to find Danny. I had been trying to keep it together, but as soon as I left Emma, I began to panic even more. *Where are you, my love? Where are you?* I kept walking down toward the beach closer to the water, frantically looking everywhere for Danny's face. I didn't recognize any of the faces there. Everything seemed to move in slow motion. *What the hell happened? What is all this?* I could see pieces of something floating on the water. I thought I recognized our boat pulled up to the beach; I could see yellow and pink (the two main colors of the Schiada) gleaming in the water, but there was too much going on and too many officers around it all to really see what was happening. Suddenly, I saw someone being taken in a gurney, and thinking it was Danny, I screamed to him, "Danny!"

But it wasn't Danny, it was Tim, Danny's co-worker and friend, the one who'd just arrived about an hour before and had met us at the beach. Tim came up for the weekend to spend some time with us and visit the river Danny had talked to him so much about. He got on the boat with the boys as soon as he'd arrived with no time for anything else. I don't even think he was wearing any beach clothes. That last damn boat ride of the day changed everything, and now he was in a gurney.

"Where's Danny?" I asked Tim. He looked at me and pointed toward the boat.

"On the boat," he said. As I ran to the boat, I could see pieces of it floating in the water; our boat was split in half. All the panic and fear I had felt in my heart up until this point had not been in vain. I knew something had gone terribly wrong. I had felt it all along. I was shaking. Tears were streaming down my face.

"Danny! Babe!" I screamed for him to hear me. "Danny!" Then I saw him, laying across the back of the boat. I recognized his blue swim trunks. I couldn't tell if or how badly he was hurt. I was about to jump into the boat when a sheriff stopped me. "I'm his wife!" I was frantic, "I need to get to my husband!"

"I'm so sorry, ma'am," he said, "there was nothing more we could—"

I didn't let the officer finish. I didn't register what he just said. I pushed through him and I jumped in the boat, finally getting to Danny. He was just lying there, not moving. Lifeless. I went to hold him, and I surveyed his entire body for visual trauma.

"Babe, it's me, I'm here." There was blood on his face, his head, and his swim trunks, but I couldn't tell where it was all coming from or where he'd gotten hurt. I couldn't see much. It was too dark. Only a light from a distant light pole overhead gave me glimpses. *Why hasn't anyone helped him?!* "Please wake up my love, I'm here." I held him and begged him to talk to me, but he wouldn't respond. I got frustrated and started to shake him, *"Please, babe, please wake up!"* Frustration turned into anger. *"Why won't you wake up?!"* I hit his face and his chest and he still wouldn't respond.

"Daniel, please wake up! Please wake up!" I was screaming over and over at him to wake up. *"Stop playing already!"* I looked around at all the people around me, staring at me. Why wasn't anyone helping me?! I eventually stopped screaming. I caressed his face and laid my head on his chest, hoping for a heartbeat.

"I love you, babe. Please don't leave me, my love, please. You can't leave us! What will I ever do without you, Daniel John? I cannot be on earth without you." I held him tight and told him I loved him over and over again until I had exhausted myself. I had no energy left. No tears left. I felt frozen, unable to move. When I leaned over to kiss him, his lips turned blue. And at that moment, I knew he was gone. My babe was gone. My husband was really gone. I had to find that out for myself. *Why had no one told me this? How could they let me find out like this?* I sat there alone on the back of the boat for what seemed forever and not enough time, Danny in my arms. This damn boat. The boat that had once brought so much joy into his life. The boat he had worked on so many nights on end. The boat that had given our family hope and so many adventures was now the boat where I held my dead husband's body. *I should have been there. It should have been me.*

I'm not sure how long I was there, sitting with Danny in my arms, but when I came up for air, everyone was gone. They took Tim to the hospital and my friend and her family were gone too; they took Emma with them. An officer came up to me and dragged me out of the boat. My white cover-up was stained with Danny's blood. I felt weak. Drained. In shock. Was this really happening? *What the fuck just happened? What the fuck happened between the time we left the beach to get started on dinner, to now?* I wanted answers, but no one would give me answers. There was still so much chaos. Night had fallen. It was now dark out and hard to see, but I did notice another wrecked boat on the beach. There were pieces of it floating in the water with ours.

"Let's take her to an ambulance," I heard an officer say. "Please take her," he said to a paramedic. Then he looked at me and said, "You are going to be ok."

I didn't want to leave Danny. I wanted to stay with my husband. I wanted to stay there forever, close to him. I was shaking and inconsolable. Filled with pain. Grief. Shock. Numbness. I felt lost. Alone. So alone. *How am I supposed to tell our daughter?*

The Long Road Ahead

How did I end up here?

The drive from the river house to back home in Lakewood was the longest drive of my life. My dad drove my car, I think, I'm not quite sure of this. My brain wasn't functioning properly enough to notice certain details. What I do remember is Emma being with me. I needed her with me at all times. She was my comfort. My person. Everything I had left. I remember just looking out the window the entire drive home. There was not much to see, really, but the blue sky, the bare trees, and a never-ending road.

I kept replaying the past few days in my head. *Didn't we just get here? We were on vacation? What just happened? How did I end up here?* Friday night after the paramedic walked me to and sat me in the back of the ambulance, I was alone, alone and devastated with a complete stranger sitting next to me, probably feeling pity for me. I didn't even know where Emma was. I knew she was with the friends we had come to the river with, but I had no idea where everyone went. Last I saw them had been in the back of the ambulance where we first saw my friend's husband and kids. By the time I was pulled away from Danny and put in the ambulance, I was alone.

I had never felt more alone. It was then, in all of my loneliness, that I had managed the courage to call Papa, Danny's dad. *How am I going to tell him? What am I going to say? I can't do this, but I have to. He needs to know.* I started looking for my phone and realized I didn't have it. *I must've dropped it when I ran to Danny.* I was freaking out, I had nothing with me. I was still half-dressed in a bathing suit and cover-up. I quickly told the paramedic I'd lost my phone; I needed my phone. *Please, I need to make a call.* I jumped out of the ambulance and started to frantically look for my phone everywhere. I was hunched almost to the floor searching every square inch of the area where I'd parked and ran. It was dark out; I'm not really sure of the time. The paramedic got out of the ambulance to try and help me, but we had no luck.

Due to the investigation and the coroner trying to do his job, I had not been allowed any closer to where Danny was anymore. He was still on the boat. I was only a few feet away from him, yet I felt so far away. I felt helpless. I couldn't find my phone. I couldn't be with Danny. I was crying. Upset. Desperate. Frantic. I disappointedly walked back to the ambulance, and a couple minutes later, an officer came in and asked, "Is this your phone?"

I managed to dial Papa's house line because that was the only number I knew by heart; we had used it many times for our discounts at Ralph's. The phone rang and no one answered, so I dialed again. It started to go to the answering machine when I heard Andrea's, Papa's wife's, voice, "Hello?" I couldn't speak. I couldn't say it out loud. If I said it out loud, that meant it was true. I didn't want this to be true. This couldn't be true. "Faby," she said, "how is it going?" She had recognized my number on the machine.

"Danny," I managed to say, "something happened." The paramedic was sitting across from me and nodded his head as if to give me courage.

"What happened, everything ok?!"

"Danny died!"

"What?!" Andrea said. "Stop playing!" She said it in a nervous but laughing manner thinking I was messing with her.

I said it again, "Danny died; there was an accident!" I couldn't speak anymore. The huge lump in my throat and pain in my heart didn't allow me to keep going. I started crying uncontrollably and handed the phone over to the paramedic. He got on the phone and explained to Andrea what had happened, what was happening, who he was, and where we were. I'm not sure exactly what else he said to her; I lost myself for a moment. The paramedic then handed me back the phone and put his hand on my shoulder. We sat there in silence, not knowing what say.

"Are you married?" I asked him.

"Yes," he replied, "and I will go home to my wife tonight and every night and love her extra hard. I will live our life as if it were my last day every day, I promise, for you. Now, let's get you out of here," he said to me. "I have to take you to the hospital."

I rode completely alone in the back of that ambulance. I cried and cried until I dry heaved with no more tears left. My life had just come crumbling down in a matter of hours. We pulled up to the hospital only a few miles from where we had started. The ride hadn't been actually long, but to me, it felt like years had gone by. The nice paramedic walked me out and asked me if I was going to be ok. I looked at him and nodded. He didn't know what else to say. What else was there to say? He then got back in the ambulance and drove off.

I walked into the hospital, a tiny hospital in the middle of no-where, with my white beach cover-up covered with Danny's blood. I must've looked like an insane person. I was shivering and felt numb all at the same time. *I hate hospitals. The last time I was in a hospital I almost died. My baby almost died. And now, my Danny is dead.*

I had no idea where I was going, but it didn't take too long be-fore I saw Emma and our friends through glass doors. They were in an exam room. Emma was sitting up on the bed with one of the kids. I walked in and hugged her tight. I didn't know what to say to her. *She is only three. How do I explain any of this to her?* Luckily for the time being, she hadn't asked me a thing; she hadn't asked me why we were there or where Daddy was. There had been so much happening so fast that there was little time for questions. I wasn't sure if she'd asked our friends anything or if they had explained anything to her.

They were busy trying to get one of their kids stitched up. He got hit in the back of the head during the incident. Poor thing was crying and in pain. But then he started to tell me about the boat hitting him, and Danny too. It was hard to hear a child recalling what he'd seen and experienced. I tried to help comfort him, but I felt so out of place. Out of body. Lost. Numb. I looked around at everyone thinking, *Do you know Danny is dead?* But of course they knew. They were in parent mode, though. They were incredibly frustrated with the hospital and the staff's lack of knowledge while trying to stitch their son up. They were talking about going to another hospital to get it done, and the elephant in the room hadn't been mentioned. *Why am I here? Why are we here? I need you, Danny!* The doctor was taking too long and everyone was restless. Finally, the couple opted to discharge their son and decided to go to the other hospital after all. I didn't know where the other hospital was; I didn't even know where we were at the moment. When the paramedic drove me, I hadn't even looked out the window to see which part of town we were going to.

Kenny, one of Danny's good friends since his high school years, suddenly showed up at the hospital. He had heard the news and was there for support. *How the hell does Kenny know? Who told him? This just happened.* I hadn't told any of his friends. I hadn't told but two people. I wasn't sure how Kenny knew or how he'd found us, but news sure traveled fast. I recalled Danny telling me once, *Kenny always seems to be at the right place at the right time.* I guess he'd been right. I liked Kenny; he had always been a good friend to Danny. They didn't talk daily or see each other too often, but Kenny was one of those friends that had always been there for Danny when he needed him. He was the one who'd told Danny about the Schiada being for sale. He was the one who'd come with us to Lake Havasu to pick up the boat. And he was also the one who'd helped Danny work on the boat to get it in tip top shape for river season. Kenny was a comforting, familiar face.

"I want to go back to Danny," I said to Kenny. I needed to go back to where Danny was, where I had last seen him. I felt lost here. I couldn't find my place. I also needed to get my car, which was where Danny was, back at the marina. Kenny and the friend he was with gladly offered to drive me. Emma stayed behind; our friends insisted she'd be better with them for now.

When we got back to the marina, I walked down toward the beach to try and see if Danny was still there, where I'd last left him, but the coroner stopped me. He asked who I was and where I was going.

"I am his wife," I said to him.

"Can I ask you a few questions?" he replied.

"Sure." He then pulled me aside and proceeded to interrogate me.

"What did you do today?"

"We were on the water most of the day. Up and down river, then we stopped at Topock66 Marina for a late lunch." Topock 66 was a restaurant on the Colorado River with amazing views. "We hung out there for a while and let the kids swim in the pool." Emma had been so happy and excited that she could finally get her tummy wet—no more feeding tube restrictions. She'd been like a little mermaid.

"Who were you with?" he continued.

"My husband, my daughter, my husband's friend and wife, and their two boys."

"Where did you go next?"

"After lunch, we packed up and headed home. We pulled up on our private beach, on Colorado Shores, five minutes from here. One of my husband's friends, Tim, came to visit, and the boys, my husband and his friend decided to take Tim on a short boat ride, last one of the night, before heading in the house. We have a house in the area. It was getting late, so my girlfriend, my daughter, and I decided to get a head start on dinner while they went on their boat ride. While making dinner, we got a very concerning call from her husband and we ended up here, to find…" I couldn't finish the sentence.

"Ok," he said, "thank you for your cooperation. I'm so sorry for your loss."

I started making my way back toward Kenny, and as I walked away, I kept looking back at the coroner's car. I knew Danny was in there. I didn't want to leave. I didn't want to leave Danny all alone. I ached for my husband. I wanted so badly to turn back time. I wanted so badly to go back to a few hours prior and change the course of the night. I wished I'd said to Danny, *Please don't go on this boat ride. Come in for the night. Let's just have dinner and enjoy this time together.* But I hadn't. And now, I couldn't.

I met back with Kenny, and we headed toward my car. Although I said I could drive myself home, Kenny insisted I shouldn't drive in my condition, so he drove me. We pulled up to the house in complete and utter silence. Upon entering the house, I noticed dinner preparations were still all over the kitchen counter. We barely managed to turn the stove off before running out the door. The evidence of what was supposed to be a great dinner night with friends was nothing but a distant memory.

It hurt. Everything hurt. This home hurt. I headed upstairs to our bedroom, closed the door, and threw myself in bed. Once alone, I allowed myself to cry as hard as I could and as loud as I needed. *This isn't happening. I didn't just lose you.* I looked around our bedroom, our stuff from when we got there the night before hadn't even been put away yet. *I am all alone. Completely alone. What the fuck just happened?!?! I should have been there! Why didn't I stop you from going on that stupid last ride?! I should've been there! If only I would've been there, maybe I could have seen something. Prevented this. I could have saved you. God, I just want to die. I want to go with you. I don't want to be here on this earth without you. You told me once you could never be on this earth without me, then why did you fuckin' leave me?! Why did you leave us?! What am I supposed to do without you?! What am I supposed to tell Emma?! Did you think about her? Did you think about me?! Why?! Why? Why?!*

I cried so hard, I dozed off for a moment, or passed out, or lost myself. I'm not sure which one. Kenny was still downstairs; he never left. I heard him come upstairs to check on me once. I am not sure when, but I remember mustering up the courage to call my mother. *How the hell do I give her news like this? What do I say?* When I heard her voice on the other end of the line, I just blurted it out, "Danny died."

I heard her almost scream, "What?!"

I repeated myself, "Danny died." And I lost it. I also called his best friend, Adam. Adam and Danny worked together at SpaceX and carpooled together every morning. *He needs to know*, I told myself. *He will miss him on Monday.* I also remember talking to Danny's boss, Chris. More than a boss, Chris was Danny's friend, our friend. Danny had just spoken to Chris prior to us making the trip. He spoke so greatly of Chris that I thought, *Chris should know; Chris will also miss him on Monday.* The thoughts that popped into my head were bizarre. It was almost like I was saying, *Hey guys, Danny won't be in on Monday, but you'll see him Tuesday.* Trauma kicks in and the brain takes control. There were moments where I was in a daze, zombie like. Then there were moments when I was aware of everything. Too aware. Other moments I expected Danny to walk through the door. We had dinner pending, of course, he knew to come to dinner. Then, reality would hit again, and I would curl up in bed wanting to die. *It should have been me. I should have been there. Why did we come here?* And I would drift off again.

As the evening went on, I heard voices which woke me up. Emma was back. It hurt to see my little girl. Although she was pretty unaware of what was happening, I wasn't. She would never get to see her Dadda again., and that broke me. I couldn't look at anyone. Everything made me sad. The room I was in, our bedroom, was tearing me apart. *This is where we last slept together, last night.* I was clinging on to one of Danny's shirts I had grabbed earlier to comfort myself. I wanted to smell him. I wanted to feel him. I had cried so much on it though, it no longer smelled like anything but my tears.

The terrible news of the accident spread like wildfire. The area there at the river where the house is isn't big and news traveled fast. *Zack News* (the local news reporter) covered the story, and by that time, everyone at the river knew what happened. Suddenly, I was receiving messages from people giving me condolences and asking me what happened. Some out of pure love and others out of morbid curiosity. Later, one by one, my family started arriving. My parents had called my siblings and they dropped everything to come be with me: my sister, my brother, and his wife. Later, my aunts, uncles, and cousins came, too. Chris, Danny's boss, had also made the drive out to the river house to show his support and be of help, something I will always be grateful for. Danny's stepbrother and his wife later showed up, too. Our house was suddenly full of people; after a while, I lost count. I kept to myself upstairs in my room most of the time. The one person I was wanting and dreading to see, was Papa. He had been on a motorcycle ride with some of his buddies, Andrea, had to get a hold of him to give him the news. I hadn't been able to talk to him at all. Papa dropped everything and made arrangements to try and get to us at the river house as quickly as possible, but his arrival felt like it took an eternity. I'm sure he felt the same. I needed Papa there with me; he loved Danny just as much as I did.

Danny's relationship with his dad was a beautiful one. More than just father and son, they were best friends, and not the way some say they are best friends, like, truly best friends. They couldn't live without each other. They called each other daily, at least once, just to check in. It was like clockwork. I used to make fun of them all the time for their predictability. Papa would call and Danny always answered with, "Hey dad!" After a while when I'd see Papa calling, I'd say, "Hey dad!" before Danny could even answer. We always got a chuckle out of that, "Babe, don't make fun of me. Did you hear that, dad? She's laughing at me again!" The father-son relationship they had was unlike any I'd ever known. It was one I hoped Danny would also have with our daughter. They never needed an excuse to call each other or work on something together or ask each other for advice. They had amazing adventures dirt bike riding, camping, tinkering in the garage, or plain sitting around and chatting away about everything and nothing.

How could I look Papa in the eyes and tell him his son was dead? What would I even say? I could barely get this fact into my own head. I was going to break his heart. His baby was gone—literally, his baby. Danny was the youngest of five children. His parents had divorced when Danny was two years old, and both his parents had remarried. Papa's children included Danny and Tim, Danny's older brother, and Andrea had three children all older than Danny.

Sometime in the late evening, Papa arrived at the house. I was upstairs in the same spot, laying in the fetal position on the bed when he walked in. I sat up when someone said, Papa is here, but I didn't say a word. I couldn't speak. I looked at him and lost it. I could see so much pain in his eyes. We just held each other and cried, cried for everything we felt and couldn't say. What could we say? We had both just lost the person we loved most in this world. I will never forget that moment. I will never forget the look on his face.

Night turned into morning, and then again. All was chaotic and calm at the same time. All I wanted was to be alone. All I wanted was to have us back, our little family of three. I couldn't find my place. I kept wandering outside to the last spot by the water where Danny and I used to sit and look out. The place where we'd had that beautiful peaceful last night together. I wished I could turn back time and get back to that moment. The moment before my life fell apart. The moment before my life broke into a million little pieces. The moment when my life and my little family was complete. *Maybe if I close my eyes and wish this all away enough, I will wake up from this horrible nightmare. I wish. I wish. I wish.* But nothing seemed to work.

It felt like years since this nightmare began. The night the coroner interrogated me and took Danny's body, he had given me no other information. We were in the dark and heard nothing more. We had no news of the whereabouts of Danny's body, when he would get transferred, or where. We'd heard the investigation would take a long time, and all we could do was wait, but wait for what?! I needed to know where my husband had been taken. *What the hell do I do now? Who do I talk to? Where do I go from here? Do I start making funeral arrangements now?* I didn't know what to do or where to start. I had only lost one other person close to me, my grandma. She died of pancreatic cancer earlier that same year, but my mother and her siblings had made all the arrangements.

After hours of calls to everyone and anyone we thought could help, trying so hard to find out where Danny's body was, we finally managed to speak to someone who would tell us and allowed us to see my husband. Papa wanted to see his Danny boy; he needed confirmation that it was really true. I needed to see my husband one more time. It was the middle of the night, and they told us we had only a few minutes—it had to be quick. Danny's stepbrother and his wife drove us to the building, it looked like a church from what I remember. Once there, a man guided us to where Danny was.

Seeing and holding Danny at the river after the accident had been incredibly difficult, full of shock and trauma, to say the least. My mind hadn't been able to wrap itself around the idea yet, but seeing my husband in a body bag is something I will never be able to describe. When the man pulled the zipper open to show us, only his head and a glimpse of his chest showed. My heart stopped. I tried so hard to pull myself together for Papa; I knew how hard this would be for him. I held my breath and tried to give him his moment, a moment I knew would change him for the rest of his life. Danny looked peaceful, if that was even possible. They had cleaned him up and on the surface, it looked like nothing ever happened, like he was just asleep. We didn't have much time, the man warned us. I caressed and kissed my Danny's head goodbye, and we walked out of there in utter silence. That was the last time I saw my husband until the funeral services.

Faby Ryan

Home

They say home is where the heart is,
but my heart was no longer with me.

My heart started to race as we got off the freeway to home. Home. I wasn't sure what that word meant anymore. Home used to be us, Faby, Danny, and Emma, the Ryans. And now, there was just Faby and Emma. It had been three days since that horrific night, three days that seemed like years. As we pulled into the driveway, I was filled with immense grief. I opened the car door and got out, but I couldn't seem to move past the front door. I stared at the house, the beautiful house we purchased and moved into only a couple months earlier. The house that was filled with dreams and hopes for a bright future ahead—our forever home, a home Emma could grow up in. A home where we'd grow old and happy. Now, it felt strange being here. I tried taking a few steps toward the door, but my body just wouldn't budge. I was shaking and couldn't stop the tears.

After what felt like forever, I finally made it to the door, turned the key, and walked into an empty house. Empty, just like my heart felt. We barely had furniture in the house; we were still in the process of moving things in. I saw the gray couches that had just been delivered on Thursday, the night we left for the river house, the night before the accident. We sat on these couches for merely five minutes, just to see what they felt like. "We'll get to really enjoy these as soon as we are back," Danny had said as I snapped a picture of my couches before heading out.

"Our home is coming along, babe; it's starting to feel like us," I replied. And we headed out. It had been a crazy year of changes for us. Within the span of five months, we sold our home, purchased and remodeled a new one, and moved our family to a city where we knew only two people. We were ready to start a new journey where our daughter could receive the tools she needed to thrive. It had been a rollercoaster of changes and sacrifices, but we had done it all together. All for our little family, and it was all worth it.

Earlier that year, in May, when Emma was close to graduating from her early intervention school in Westchester, CA, at the age of three, they talked to us about the next steps in Emma's school career. Because Emma had been special ed her entire life, she needed services and therapies like speech therapy, occupational therapy, physical therapy, early intervention therapy, oral therapy, and whatever else came our way. She would continue to need these services, so Emma would need a Special Education School and would be provided an IEP or Individualized Education Program. An IEP is a legal document given to public schools for K-12 children with disabilities. The disability has to be legally recognized. The document outlines specific learning needs and goals so that the child can receive the proper attention, instruction, support, and services they need to thrive in school.

At this point, I had already learned so much through regional center (a non-profit that helps find access to available services for individuals with disabilities), scheduling Emma's therapies, and even ordering all her medical equipment over the phone, but this IEP stuff was a new ball game and incredibly overwhelming. Once they started mentioning lawyers and binding documents, the stress became real. Plus, I would no longer have the assistance or personal support from Blanca, my regional center go-to. I was on my own. I started searching for schools in our area that could provide everything our daughter needed, but the school district where we lived was very small and they didn't know much about situations like ours. This was when I started researching other options for us. One of Emma's therapists, Marlyna, had mentioned Long Beach had an incredible school district that largely provided special ed programs for children like Emma. The more I did my research, the more I confirmed Long Beach was where we needed to be.

One day, I came home from one of these prep meetings and I said to Danny, "Babe, we are moving to Long Beach!"

"What?" he replied. "What do you mean moving to Long Beach?" Once I explained to him the situation, what I'd learned, and what Emma needed, he was all in. "Anything for our little love," he said. We had worked so incredibly hard with therapies and early intervention to get Emma where she was, and we would continue to do anything in our power to get her thriving even more. We were hopeful that eventually, her diagnoses of being "delayed" would be a thing of the past, and she would no longer need special schools or special services. Emma was a thriving and incredibly smart little girl, but as long as she needed extra support, we would provide her with any and all the help/assistance we could, even if that meant moving to a new city.

With Emma graduating early intervention, and a new school and IEPs hanging over our heads, we decided to move forward with hunting for a new house. One Sunday in mid-March, Danny and I decided to go check out this open house in the city of Lakewood. The house was in a good neighborhood where we knew a couple people. And one of the schools I had researched for Emma, which was perfect for her, was not too far. We pulled up to the house and Danny was instantly discouraged. Our first home had been a tiny little fixer-upper, and we had put so much work into it that the last thing Danny wanted was yet another fixer-upper.

"Let's just look at it," I said. "We have nothing to lose." As we walked into the house, I saw Danny cringe. This house needed so much work, and while Danny was always the optimist in these scenarios and I, the pessimist, this time around, we switched roles.

"I see potential," I said.

"Potential? Are we both seeing the same house?" Danny replied.

The house, although it had gone through a remodel years before, seemed old and unkept. As we toured the house, every room became more and more… colorful. Each room had a different colored carpet—orange, pink, green. The galley kitchen seemed small as it was filled top to bottom with old looking brown cabinets. The front living room had a brick fireplace that extended way too far into the center of the room, which made the room seem smaller and unnecessary. The master bedroom had been an add-on, and although not aesthetically pleasing, it was quite large and nice. It had his and hers walk-in closets, which made me do a little dance, and a master bathroom—score! The two upstairs bedrooms were decent sizes and had a shared bathroom in the hallway. This seemed ideal as Danny and I were considering having another baby. I knew what Danny was thinking the entire time, *This is way too much work*, but I kept seeing potential.

"This will be a ton of work to redo, but I think we can do it!" I said in excitement. Danny wasn't used to my optimism when it came to a house remodel and dirty work, but he knew together, we could do it. So, he went with it, always wanting to make his girls happy.

"Ok, babe, I'll call our broker and let her know we are interested in the house and want to put an offer on it," he said.

I looked at him with disbelief and excitement. Were really doing this? Since we wanted this home purchase to be as smooth as possible, we decided to hire the seller's realtor as our own, hoping it would move things faster.

Sue, the seller of the house lived by herself. Her husband had died years prior while on a vacation. *How sad*, I said to Danny, *can you imagine?!* Sue wanted to sell and move back to San Francisco to be with her children; it made no sense to her to live in this big house alone. She was more than ready to sell, which worked to our advantage. We left the house really considering putting in an offer. Worst case scenario, they didn't accept it. *But what if they did?*

On our way home, we called Nancy, our broker, and got things moving. We had already been preapproved for a loan, so we got the ball rolling pretty quickly. Less than a week later, we put an offer on the house. Not long after that, we had an answer. Danny called me from work one Monday morning and said, "You better be ready, babe, 'cause we just bought a house!"

"What? Stop messing with me!" I said.

"Babe, we just bought a house; they accepted our offer!"

On March 19th, right before my 32nd birthday, we toasted with a cheap bottle of champagne as we signed the buyer agreement. We knew this would be a stressful time, but Danny and I made a great team. When times were tough, we knew how to tag team the responsibilities and lean on each other to ease some of the stress. We learned this the hard way, especially after having Emma. *What's gonna work? Teamwork!* I can still hear Danny saying this in song form.

Time was of the essence, and we needed to get to work. Our current house needed some aesthetic work done to get ready to be put on the market. It was not much as we'd done a lot of work to the house over the last six years, but it was work nonetheless. I also had to temporarily enroll Emma in our local school so she could continue therapy services; we did not want her regressing on her progress and met goals. I quickly met with an IEP team at the local school to go over Emma's medical assessment, needs, and required services that would be provided so that as soon as she graduated from early start, her transition into the school system would flow smoothly.

While Emma was progressing, she still had health issues and many hurdles to get though. Just earlier that month she had been in the hospital for almost a week with severe pneumonia and infection. We, as well as the school staff had to be incredibly careful with handling her care. Emma still had a feeding tube at this point and the school didn't know much about it; so, I went to meet with the school nurse and train her on how to change her feeding tube in case of an emergency.

"No matter what ever happens with Emma, please call me! I am only down the street!" I reiterated over and over. Handing over this responsibility to someone who wasn't familiar with Emma's case made me extremely anxious. All the therapists who had worked with Emma up until this point had been with her since we'd come home from the NICU. These people would be new to her case.

Emma graduated early intervention on May 1st 2015, two days before her third birthday. The school had an exit celebration for her and a few of her other graduating friends, royal blue cap and all. Our baby looked incredibly beautiful, and we were filled with so much pride. Our little girl had worked so hard up until this point, and there was no stopping her. After the graduation at her school, Danny and I took her out to celebrate. She wanted sushi, her favorite food then (and now).

On May 18th, our new property in Lakewood closed escrow, and on May 22nd, we got the keys to our new home. Danny and I celebrated the occasion by borrowing some champagne glasses from a new neighbor and popping a bottle of champagne in the middle of our empty, pink-carpeted living room. Emma ran throughout the entire empty house excitedly as we toasted. It was perfect. By the end of that week, the gutting of the house and remodel had begun. On May 31st, we listed our first home for sale. Danny and I had purchased that home the same year we got married. It was the home where we became a family of three. It was difficult to think we would be letting that place go. There were so many emotions as we saw the for sale sign go up. That house held so many memories, and even though it is no longer my house, I still drive by it sometimes.

Emma started attending our local school and she was really enjoying it. She loved her teacher and was acclimating well to the temporary change. The school was great with her. They were incredibly loving and attentive to her needs; I was actually starting to get attached to this little team we had built, but I knew we wouldn't be there long. Things with the house were moving along, and we were working on getting it ready and presentable to start showing. The Ryans were moving! I wish things had been as easy as that sounds, but the stress of it all was real.

Our house sold pretty quickly, quicker than we ever imagined. Within five days of putting it on the market, our house sold. In any other case, this would have been ideal, but with our new property being completely gutted and in the middle of a remodel, this meant we had exactly thirty days to get it all done! Our goal was to have the new place done and ready to move in by the weekend of the Fourth of July. Needless to say, that didn't happen. As life would have it, the remodel had its hiccups and it was taking longer than expected. We ended up having to crash at Danny's dad's house for a couple weeks. He didn't mind; any and all time spent with Danny and Emma was ok by him. But Danny wasn't a big fan of staying anywhere other than home. Home to him was a sacred space.

On July 12th, with the help of some of Danny's friends, we officially moved our stuff into the new house. Well, the garage and back porch, that is. Nonetheless, we were making headway, and that was a win. On July 15th, in the middle of house remodel chaos, we celebrated Danny's 36th birthday. Nothing fancy. Danny never really cared about parties or material things. He just wanted us to be together. And on July 17th, he got the perfect gift: we officially moved into our new home. It wasn't completely done or furnished yet, but we were finally in. On August 8th, in a barely furnished home, we hosted our friends, family, and some of our new neighbors at a housewarming party. It was perfect. In early September, Emma started at her new school, Buffum Total Learning Center, in Long Beach—the main reason we upped and moved our lives to this new city.

And now, here I stood, in the house where we hoped to make new memories. In the place we couldn't wait to call home. Alone. I stood in silence in the middle of my living room, staring at those gray couches we never got to sit in together. I could hear Danny's voice telling me, "Babe, we'll get to enjoy these as soon as we are back!" We had made plans that would never come. He had made promises he hadn't been able to keep. My husband was gone, and I was all alone and broken. How was I supposed to carry on all on my own? How would I ever be able to look at this house the same? I walked into my bedroom and locked myself in the bathroom as my parents and Danny's parents walked in the house. There was silence. So much silence. No one knew what to say or do. Once in my room, I sobbed all the tears I had held in on the never-ending car ride home.

Services

Daniel John Ryan
July 15, 1979 – October 9, 2015

The day after we arrived back home, I had an appointment at a cemetery close to home in Long Beach, CA. I had looked it up on-line and it looked decent, whatever the hell that meant. Upon arrival, we were greeted by a coordinator who looked at me with pity in their eyes.

"I'm so very sorry for your loss," they said.

"Thanks," I said as I was handed a book with packages and prices which I briefly looked through. It had flowers, displays, head-stones—the works. I didn't know what I was supposed to do or say. It was awkward, it felt out of body. I got asked a bunch of questions about Danny: what happened, where his body was. His body hadn't even been transferred yet; it was still in San Bernardino County. The coroner wouldn't release his body until the investigation was conclud-ed, so technically, we couldn't even plan for actual services yet. We just had to have everything in place for when his body was ready to be transferred to whichever place I decided on. These questions were overwhelming and irritating.

When we finally got started with a tour of the place, we walked around the facility as the coordinator yapped and yapped. I suddenly found myself standing in the middle a room that displayed caskets of all sizes and finishes. Staring at me were some hideous gold and gaudy ones Danny would have thrown up at the sight of; I could almost hear him laughing.

I suddenly felt like I was about to lose it. I tried to control my-self. *I can't lose it. Papa and Andrea are with me, also Danny's stepbrother and his wife—I don't need them to see me falling apart.* We continued on with the tour and walked through a stupid room which nicely dis-played wedding-like signature books, photos, and programs. *I wonder if these people in the photos actually died. I need to get out of here. What the fuck am I doing here?! Why is this person talking to me like we are planning a fucking party?!* I started to feel irritated. Emotional. Angry.

The last place I wanted to be in was here. *Never in my wildest dreams did I ever think I'd be planning my husband's funeral.* The place wasn't big, so covering the grounds didn't take long, but to me, it felt like an eternity. Last but not least, we were taken to the available grave sites. Touring and choosing grave sites was just like touring and choosing a home, all business. Except in this case, it was real estate I never wished for nor wanted. I was so ready to get out of there. "I don't think this is the place," I said. "This doesn't feel like the right place." *But what the fuck is it I'm supposed to feel?! How am I supposed to make a decision like this? How do I decide where I want to "lay to rest" my dead husband?* I was drained and just wanted to go home.

★ ★ ★

The next morning, I had another meeting at a cemetery in Rancho Palos Verdes, CA. I held beautiful memories of Rancho Palos Verdes: Danny and I had often gone on long romantic drives along the coast. Hiking and mountain biking in the hills had been one of our favorites, too; we even had a "secret bench." Rancho Palos Verdes was the place where we'd had our wedding reception, at beautiful Point Vicente Interpretive Center. I used to tell Danny that when I died, because obviously I would go first, to cremate me and throw my ashes off the cliff there. But now, here I was planning *his* services. *How could you have left me? I was supposed to go first.*

I had never been to Green Hills Cemetery; I never even knew it existed. Death and cemeteries were not something I'd experienced much of, aside from my grandma, but she'd been buried elsewhere. Green Hills is huge and has a calming vibe to it. Maybe it's the pond near the hills and mini waterfall with its calming water sounds that make it feel peaceful. Or maybe it's being in the hills away from the city that gives it that feeling. I wasn't sure what it was, but this place was nice.

After touring and chatting with Lori and Rob, the coordinators at Green Hills Cemetery and mortuary, I decided this would be the place where I laid my husband to rest. It made sense. It felt right. I chose a casket: a simple, yet nice one with a wood finish, one I knew Danny would've liked, as if that mattered—but to me it did. I picked a grave site near the pond and waterfall overlooking a cute white chapel. I figured Danny would've liked the calming water sounds, and I would, too, when I came to visit. And whether I wanted it or not, I had to purchase a grave site for two; they don't sell singles. So, I now have a place where I will be buried next to my husband someday. It had been a long day, but I managed to make all the arrangements I wished I never had to make, and with an almost forty-thousand-dollar bill, I walked out of there. I was depleted. Overwhelmed. But also I was relieved this part was done and off my shoulders. "This was the easy part," Rob had said, the worst days were yet to come.

Daniel John Ryan
July 15, 1979 – October 9, 2015
Daniel John Ryan, the son of Valerie Reyburn and Michael Ryan, passed away October 9, 2015, at the age of 36. He was born on July 15, 1979, in California. Daniel is survived by his loving wife, Faby Ryan and daughter Emma Ryan. Viewing will be held on Friday October 23, 2015, from 5-9 pm at Green Hills Memorial Chapel in Rancho Palos Verdes. Services will be held on Saturday October 24, 2015, at St. Lawrence Martyr Church at 10 am in Redondo Beach followed by burial service at Green Hills Cemetery.

Friday, October 23, 2015

I didn't trust myself to drive, so I asked Adam and Nicki, our friends, if they could please pick Emma and me up and drive us to Green Hills for the viewing service. I figured I could always catch a ride back home with someone. They graciously agreed to drive us. The drive was quiet. None of us knew what to say. I didn't know how to feel. On the outside, I looked fine. I had put myself together after weeks of not caring what I looked like. I wore heels, and a floral black dress I'd had sitting in my closet unworn for years. My hair went from being in a bun for days to actually looking decent. But on the inside, I was a mess—completely broken. I wanted to look presentable for Danny, though; this would be the last time I would physically see him.

I had reserved some alone time at the chapel for Emma and me before the rest of the family could come in. I wanted the three of us together, just us. My heart was pounding as we arrived at the chapel. I walked up to the glass doors where I saw family already there; I honestly can't tell you who. I remember walking in, grabbing Emma by the hand, taking a deep breath, and looking up at the end of the long chapel. There, at the very end, was Danny. I started to walk very slowly as I gathered strength. I wanted to run to him, but just as much, I wanted to never get there. I wanted to see him so badly, but also, I never wanted to see him, not like this. My heart was pounding out of my chest. Tears were streaming down my face like floodgates had just opened, and suddenly, I was standing in front of his casket.

Everything I had chosen was rightly done. The brown wooden casket was perfectly polished. I had dressed Danny in his favorite brown dress shirt with horizontal blue stripes; dark brown, almost black, pinstriped dress pants that made his booty look really good; and although you couldn't see from the waist down, I had asked them to place his favorite rainbow sandals on his feet. This man had loved and lived in sandals, and this was not going be the exception.

"Oh, my love, what the fuck?!" I said as I reached my hand in to touch his face. "*What the fuck*?!" I caressed his hair and leaned in to give him a kiss. Emma tugged at my dress to pick her up, but I was a little afraid of what she might feel, do, think, say.

I picked Emma up and right away she said, "Mommy, why is Dadda so old?!"

"He's not old, my love, he just looks old." Time stood still. I'm not sure how long we stood there. I brought a picture of Emma and me to put in the casket, *So you never forget us, my love*. I placed the photo with him, caressed his hands, his face, his hair, his lips. I didn't know what to do with myself. I wished he'd open his eyes. I wished I could crawl in that casket and feel his embrace. I couldn't seem to separate myself from him. I felt so broken. After some time, I leaned in to kiss him. Emma also gave him a kiss on the forehead, and we walked out to let everyone else in.

The chapel filled with people immediately. Family. Close friends. Co-workers. Doctors and nurses from Emma's NICU. Old friends I hadn't seen in years. Old friends of Danny's I had never met. Friends of friends. Family's family. It's funny how fast news travels when someone dies, and how quickly people show up, even if you haven't seen them in years, even if they've never met you. Hundreds of people came and gave their condolences.

I remember bits and pieces from the service. The memorial video I'd put together was beautiful. There were some amazing moments there of Danny's childhood, moments with friends, moments with us, and beautiful Emma milestones. During the video playing, Emma got up and started dancing in the middle of the room saying, "Dadda." It was beautiful and made me feel better about having her there. I hadn't been sure if I'd made the right decision. I wasn't sure how this would affect her, but after speaking to a few counselors, it was suggested that I should have her there with me.

For the rest of the service, I was in and out of it. I experienced all of the stages of grief in a matter of hours. I was sad for Papa; he'd lost his son, his best friend. I was sad for me. I was sad for Emma; she would never get to grow up with her Dadda. I was in denial that Danny was laying there in a casket and there was nothing I could do about it. I was angry that Danny's mother hadn't come to the service but did send someone to drop off some poem to hand off to everyone. I felt guilt for being alive. I would have given anything to be able to trade places with Danny. I cried. I smiled. I greeted. I hugged. I shook hands. I couldn't sit still. Yet, I wanted to disappear. And when I didn't think things could get any worse, there she was, standing in front of me, the woman my husband had an affair with.

I recognized her. I don't think she realized I did. I stood there in shock, my heart pounding as she shook my hand and said, "You don't know me, but I knew your husband." She shook hands with the people standing next to me (who clearly knew her).

As she walked away, I looked over to the person next to me and asked, "Who was that?" I needed confirmation. When he said her name, I went cold inside. I just stood there, shaking, heart pounding out of my chest. If the room had been quiet enough, I'm sure they'd have been able to hear my heart. Not wanting to make a scene, I headed to the restrooms. *Is this really happening? Not only am I sitting in a room where my dead husband is laying but the woman he fucked had the audacity to show up here? Did she really think I wouldn't figure out who she was? Did she really think I was that stupid? Does she really think she has a right to be here? Who the fuck does she think she is?*

I was filled with anger. How dare she? How dare he? Tears of anger streamed down my face. I didn't want them. I didn't want to shed anymore tears over this. I tried to compose myself, but how much composure can one have in this scenario? I wanted to go find her. I wanted to scream at her. I wanted to shout at her to leave. I wanted everyone to know what a fucked-up person she was. I wanted everyone to know who she really was and what she had done to me. I wanted her true face revealed. I wanted everyone to feel the hate and anger I felt toward her, too. But I couldn't. *Not here. Not now.* I composed myself and went back out there, into the room we all stood in, my dead husband, his lover, and I.

I walked back out to the chapel, my eyes screening for her, but I no longer saw her. The room was filled with too many people to count. I walked up to my husband's casket and stared at him for what felt like forever. Time stood still. *What am I doing here? Is this really my fucking life? Can somebody please wake me up from this nightmare already? I just want to wake up. Somebody please wake me up!* When I walked back to the pews, people figured my newly swollen red eyes were because I'd had "another moment."

All I wanted to do was disappear. The rest of the night was a daze. I was trying to stay calm and composed. Some of the women friends had brought little travel bottles of wine to the chapel, just in case I needed one. I remember walking to the restroom and chugging one; I just wanted to numb the pain. I wanted to feel nothing. I wanted to forget. But nothing was working. The night had been long and painful in more ways than I could ever put into words. I'm not quite sure how it all ended or how I got home. I was exhausted and was dreading yet another day of this heart-wrenching pain of saying goodbye that awaited me the following day.

Saturday, October 24, 2015
Morning soon came. I slept very little. I kept busy working on last minute arrangements and making sure I had things situated for the service and the reception that followed. I had been dreading nighttime. Nights were the hardest. I hated climbing into an empty bed. I still hadn't been able to touch his side of the bed. Although I knew his side was empty, reaching for the space where he used to lay and finding no one there was more than I could bear. I woke up tired, worn out. But I had to put on my brave face and face the day. My sister bought me a black dress to wear because I hadn't even thought to get one. Little black dress—what a different concept that was from what I'd always known it to be. Emma wore an off-white and gold dress she had previously worn to a wedding we went to. That dress reminded me of happier days. I had a picture of Danny holding Emma in this dress; they both looked extremely happy. I wanted to hold on to that feeling.

When we arrived at St. Lawrence Martyr Church, my heart had a déjà vu moment. Once upon a time, I arrived at this very same church, dressed in white, with an eagerness to marry the man of my dreams. When those church doors opened, I saw my future husband standing there at the end of that very long aisle, we said our I dos, and scurried away toward our happily ever after. After ten months of wedding planning every single detail to perfection, the day had finally arrived. I was incredibly nervous, but never had a doubt in my mind that Danny was the one. It had not even been two minutes into my walking down the aisle before I was already in tears. I was filled with emotion and a pouring of love. I stared at Danny's eyes the entire walk, and when I finally reached the altar, my heart felt at ease.

It was a long, but beautiful, traditional Catholic wedding. I cried as we said our vows while Danny tenderly wiped my tears. I could see tears welling up in his eyes, too. And we laughed at the part where the priest forgot to say, *You may now kiss your bride.* Danny and I looked at each other like, *Do we kiss? Or do we not?* We finally looked at the priest and asked, "Can we kiss now?!" Everyone in the church laughed with us as we kissed and sealed our marriage. "We did it!" we said, and we walked out of the church holding hands, hearts soaring in love.

I stood at the steps of the church frozen in time. *Happily ever afters don't exist. This is not the ending we deserved.* I grabbed Emma by the hand and walked up to the church doors to meet some of the family already standing outside. And when I turned to look for the church coordinator, I saw "her" standing outside the church, too. *Are you kidding me?* Once again, my heart started pounding. My hands started to shake. I was instantly pissed off. *I will not allow this, not today!* I didn't even think twice. With adrenaline rushing through my body, I started to walk toward her. I wasn't even sure what I wanted to say, but I did know I would not stay silent this time. I had stayed silent for too long; I never told a soul. I had kept this secret buried in my heart and to myself for years, and it was eating me alive.

I'd felt stupid. Naïve. I hadn't wanted anyone to know of Danny's betrayal. I'd wanted to protect him, his reputation, and our marriage. I hadn't wanted to give people a reason to talk. I'd wanted to avoid the outside noise, and not allow people's opinions into my marriage. And all for what? Who had I been saving the whole time? What about my feelings? My pain? I thought this was all behind me, but there I was, standing at my husband's fucking funeral eating my anger, feeling like a fool all over again. *The stupid wife.* I didn't want to make a scene, but I did want to confront her, that is all I knew.

I walked up to her, stood in front of her with my pounding heart and my shaky voice and I said her name, "You and I both know who you are and what you've done. I do not want you here!"

She replied with something in the sense of "I am not going anywhere." *The balls!* I repeated myself and again told her I didn't want her there. And I walked away. I couldn't say more. Everything hurt. I didn't look back. I was still shaking. I expected her to leave. I expected her to have enough respect for me, my daughter, and even Danny, to leave. *Had he not made it very clear?* Danny told her he NEVER wished to see nor speak to her ever again; he forwarded me the email. To my surprise, she didn't leave. *Did she not understand what never meant?* I heard she'd gone crying to family and friends playing the victim. They'd all comforted her and probably thought what an asshole I was. Little did people know what she was doing *to me.* I couldn't believe her audacity. I couldn't believe how in the worst moments of my life she'd thought only of herself and no one else. If that wasn't selfish, I didn't know what was. For the rest of my life, when I think of those last moments with my husband, I will always feel anger at the disrespect.

I went back to find Emma since we were getting ready for service to start. Most people had already gone inside the church. I held Emma tight and lined up outside the church as they brought the casket out. The closed casket with my husband inside it. I wanted to rip it open. I wanted to see him. Hold him. Caress his face one more time. But all I could do was place my hands on top of the casket. I picked up Emma and held her in my arms as we stood in the foyer about to walk in. I stared down the long aisle, the aisle I had walked once before, almost exactly six years ago. Six years ago, when life had been beautiful.

I walked down the aisle, casket before me. I focused my eyes in front of me the entire time; I was afraid that if I looked elsewhere, or at anyone, I would crumble. Every step felt like I was walking in slow motion. The energy around me was so strong and heavy; I could feel all eyes on me. My heart was pounding so hard, I could hear my every heartbeat. The more I walked, the tighter I hugged Emma close to my body, until we reached the altar. Once at the altar, I sat in the front right pew with my husband's casket to my left. I kept my eyes focused upfront, unable to look away. Unable to move. Barely able to breathe. I stared at the altar before me, that beautiful altar where we'd laughed and kissed, smiled and cried, the altar where we'd made promises and said vows to each other. We were filled with joy and hope of our future together, and I couldn't help but question God. *Why him? Why us? Why me?*

I don't remember much about exiting the church. I think the pain inside me blocked it all. I don't remember the drive to the burial site either. It is still a fog. I do remember we released beautiful monarch butterflies as a spiritual symbol for life after death. I helped Emma with hers, and the butterfly that she was trying to release wouldn't leave her sight; it did not want to fly away. After a few attempts, it finally took flight and flew as if to the heavens. It was beautiful. There were butterflies everywhere. Butterflies, when released, can represent the deceased's soul fluttering into the afterlife and hope for the future. Hope. I wasn't sure I had any hope left in me.

As I stood there before my husband's casket, knowing this was the last time I would be able to physically see him, I remember thinking, *If I really wanted to and tried hard enough, I bet I could open that casket right this moment. I just need a little bit of courage.* My brain wanted to figure out a way to bring Danny back. Although I stood there staring at his casket about to be lowered into the ground, it all felt surreal, like I was looking into someone else's life. This had to be a dream. I stood there. I watched it all happen. I had requested to be there until the end. This was the only way I could see for myself that this was, in fact, real. I placed a white rose on top of the casket as it was about to be lowered, and I watched it descend in slow motion. I witnessed the machines cover his casket with dirt; my body was unable to move. I stood there and had no control over what was happening. I wanted my husband back and yet, this was the end of the end. After the dirt was fully packed in, they replaced the grass on top, like nothing ever happened.

I kept it together the entire service. Although inside, I wanted to scream. I wanted to throw myself over the casket and have them bury me with him. I wanted to feel free to release all the sadness and anger

I felt inside, but I wouldn't allow myself to. I wanted everyone to disappear. I wanted to be alone in my pain. Instead, I stood there, trying to be strong. Looking brave. Composed. I couldn't fall apart. Emma was counting on me, looking to me for comfort. I had to stay strong. For Emma. For Danny. Even for me.

It was a beautiful service, or so people said. I couldn't really tell you much more. Some things are hard to remember, some things, I chose not to remember.

After the burial, a reception followed. The reception was held at a car museum in Torrance, California, which held roughly 150 people. This was the amount of people who came to the service. Family. Friends. SpaceX co-workers. All who knew and loved my Danny had come to pay their respects. The reception was generously and lovingly put together by Chris, Jenny, and their assistant, Meream. They were the planners when I couldn't be. They took care of every single detail just the way I would have if I'd had the heart to. They were God-sent and an incredible support system. Jenny had only come to me with four simple questions: Danny's favorite color, flower, drink, and food. And just like magic, they turned the place into a beautiful room full of Danny's favorite things. It was Perfection.

The tables were covered in red, his favorite color. The center pieces were made up of fragrantly blooming white roses, our favorite. For dinner, a taco bar, Danny's absolute favorite food. And for drinks, his number one go-to beer, Firestone 805. And because it was at a car museum, Emma had all the space to run around and play with the cars. Papa, Chris, and even Gwynne, the President at SpaceX, took turns entertaining her so that I could have some moments to myself.

The room quickly filled, and I couldn't tell you who everyone was. I just remember faces. I found a seat at a table and plopped myself down. Many shared anecdotes of the roles Danny had played in their lives. Others shared the ways in which Danny had inspired them and/or changed them. There were funny stories, inspiring stories, some laughter, cheers, and lots of tears. And then it was my turn to speak. I hadn't yet had the courage to speak at any of the earlier services. I'd kept to myself, but at this moment I felt I should say a few words and thank everyone for their love, support, and help through this incredibly hard time.

My heart was pounding and I was crying before I could even speak. As I looked around the room, my heart became overwhelmed. I could feel everyone's stare. Up until this point, I hadn't been able to publicly speak about my loss. I had been purposefully hiding and protecting myself from the reality and the pain. And here I was, facing my biggest fear: saying it out loud. I tried to speak, but the words wouldn't come out. Somewhere in between tears and fear, I managed to say, "Thank you all for coming and being here with us. Danny would be so proud to see all of you here, to know of all of the support you have given Emma and me…" I didn't say too much more. I couldn't say much at all. I held Emma as she said into the mic, "I love you, Dadda!" and I don't remember much after that. We made a toast to an amazing human, husband, dad, son, brother, friend, and co-worker. It was a great sight to see everyone with an 805 in hand toasting to my husband. It was beautiful and touching. I wished Danny could have been there to experience it all.

Broken

I cannot be on this earth without you
Love, me.

This next part of my story is one I wish never happened. One I wish I could erase from my memory bank and dump deep in the ocean where it could never surface again. Unfortunately, this part of my story did happen, and it is a part of my story I have never talked about openly, one I've kept secret for twelve years like a message in a bottle, floating in the ocean, never to be found. It was eating me up, boiling like a pot of hot water ready to overflow any minute. The thing about secrets, though, is they don't allow us to heal. I haven't been able to heal. I have kept this buried inside my soul for so long to protect my husband's name, our marriage, an image. I didn't want to give people something to talk about, and I felt ashamed. Growing up, I was always told, *Whatever happens in the home, stays in the home. No one needs to know your dirty laundry*. And I did just that. I tried to bury this secret just like I had my husband, but the truth is, it has eaten me alive for years, especially after Danny's death when things resurfaced and I was triggered but kept quiet. I buried my husband, my feelings, my pain, and my dignity all in order to protect others. But, who ever protected me?

When someone dies, that person somehow becomes larger than life, put on a pedestal. God-like. Perfect. Someone who's never made mistakes or failed. No one ever goes to a funeral and says, "Man, that guy was an asshole!" Even if he was, they will talk about all the good parts and somehow forget the rest. That guy could suddenly do no bad, and if anyone mentions any of the bad, that person's the asshole. Truth is, no one is perfect. Dead or alive. What is perfect anyway? I know my husband wasn't perfect, and I've never made him out to be. Or maybe I have, I don't know. What I do know is who my husband was and who he wasn't.

My husband was a man with the most incredible heart. A man who loved deeply. A kind and gentle human, the most giving kind. A forgiving man. The smartest and most hardworking man I ever met. A man who could make me laugh even when I was absolutely irate. A stubborn man, equal to me. A man who had childhood trauma he had worked so much to heal, trauma no one knew about. A man who was willing to be there for anyone who needed him, no questions asked. A man who loved me and his daughter more than anyone in this world, no question. And, my husband was also a man who wasn't perfect. A man who made mistakes. A man who had made the biggest mistake of his life—his words.

A year and a half into my marriage, a beautiful time in our life, a time when I thought we couldn't be happier, still in our honeymoon phase, life slapped me in the face. One night, while looking for an email link on my husband's work computer, per his request, I discovered something of a red flag in his email inbox. The more I scrolled searching for this link, the more I kept seeing this particular email address and name, over and over. Now, up to this point I had never—I mean never—had a trust issue with my husband. I never questioned nor doubted him. I was never a jealous person to begin with. I had complete and utter trust in him. I had been cheated on in the past in my previous relationships, but with Danny, I never thought I'd have a reason to doubt him. That was, until this moment. Until these emails and the feeling in my gut.

I suddenly got this terrible feeling in my stomach that something wasn't right. I felt panic in my heart. *Don't get ahead of yourself, Faby, it might be one of the purchasing agents from work; most of his purchasing agents are women,* I told my head, but my gut feeling told me different. My heart started to race, my hands started to shake, something was off. The more I scrolled through emails, the more concerned I got. Finally, concern became panic. My heart was pounding harder and louder than any drum I'd ever heard. I felt heat rush through my entire body as I clicked the name on one of the emails. Upon opening the first one, I could immediately tell something wasn't right. *These are personal emails.* I scrolled back in his history looking for evidence that what I was seeing and feeling was a figment of my imagination. But to my disappointment, my gut was right. The more I scrolled, the more I discovered. There they were, all the emails that detailed their affair. Months of email exchanges dating over a year back. *What the fuck am I reading? This can't be right! Danny would never!* I continued to read the messages, one after another in disbelief.

At first, they seemed innocent, *hey, just wanted to say hello, how have you been?* But as the thread grew longer, they became more and more indicative of something more. *Bean burrito,* his nickname to her I guessed, *I think of you often.* Every email I read was a stab in the heart. *When can I see you again? I miss you.* This woman was in love with my husband. *It hurts me to know you are not well. I wish I could take care of you. How is your son?* Tears start streaming down my face. *I am sorry I couldn't answer you; I was away for the weekend. When can we talk?* I stared at the date; this was the weekend we were away in Santa Barbara celebrating my birthday. *Now I understand why he was acting like such an asshole—he couldn't answer her messages!* I was overcome with pain. Anger. Disbelief. Questions. Disappointment. *My husband is having an affair!* This was the moment my world fell apart for the first time. Shattered into a million pieces.

I wiped my tears and decided to call Danny; I had to hear it from him. I needed to know the truth from his own mouth. He was at a launch party for his work celebrating a successful launch of one of the rockets he'd been working on.

"Hi babe," he said as he answered the other end of the line. I could hear a bunch of noise in the background, but I didn't care.

I composed myself and I asked, "Daniel, have you ever cheated on me?"

"What babe? I can't hear you, there's a lot of noise here, hold on," he said.

He walked over to a quieter place, and I asked again, "Have you ever cheated on me, Daniel?"

"No," he replied.

"I'm gonna ask you one last time, are you cheating on me, Daniel John?"

"No." But now I could hear nervousness in his voice.

"Then what the fuck is all this I am reading, and who the fuck is this woman?!"

I couldn't hold it in any longer and I started to fall apart. I was a screaming and crying mess of a woman searching for answers.

"I'm so sorry, my love. I'm sorry. It meant nothing. She means nothing!"

I hung up the phone. I couldn't hear his voice any longer. *It's true. It's fucking true. Our entire marriage has been a lie. This is not the man I married. How could he?* He called me back. I didn't answer. He called again; I didn't answer. The third time he called, I answered, and the only thing I could think to say was "Fuck you!" And I hung up again. My world had crumbled in a matter of seconds. I cried until I no longer had tears left. My fairy tale had turned into a nightmare. It must've been four in the morning, and he was still calling. I was away, not home. Thank God I hadn't been home, I don't know what I would've done if I had been. The blinding rage and pain I felt were too much to bear.

I started questioning myself: *Was I not enough? What was wrong with me? Was I not pretty enough? Attractive enough? What was missing? What is wrong with me? What did I do? What didn't I do? I thought we were perfect?!* Why is it that when we get hurt or betrayed, the first person we question is ourselves?

The following day, we finally talked. I wanted to talk. I wanted to know everything. I needed to know everything. I'm not sure why. I knew what I would hear would only hurt more, but I needed to know it all. Maybe because I felt like I'd been in the dark for so long. I needed answers. If I was ever to forgive him, I wanted the truth, all of it, even if it hurt me. This woman had been a high school girl-friend; she emailed him months before out of nowhere to "see how he was" and that started the back and forth of emails and messaging. This wasn't the first time this occurred; through the years she would randomly "check in on him" and had been his hook up. "It was a physical thing," he said. *Fucking go-go dancer*, I thought. I had looked her up online. *What a disgusting piece of shit you messed around with.* I was angry with her for being a woman and not caring enough to ruin another, to ruin a relationship. A marriage. I wanted to hate her. I was so angry at her, but more than hating *her*, I hated what she had done, to me and to my marriage. Why couldn't she have left him alone? She knew he was in a committed relationship. I wanted to hate him. I was angry at him for betraying my trust. For hurting me in the worst possible way. For hurting our marriage. He had broken us.

How could you do this? How did this happen? When did you see her? Who picked who up? Where did you go? Where was I? I wanted to know everything to the last detail. I wanted to know when it was that he'd thought his stupid wife wouldn't suspect or know a thing.

One night while I was at work, she'd picked him up at our home, *our home*, and they went to dinner by the beach at some Cajun place. And after dinner, they fucked in the back seat of her car, in a nutshell. I don't know what hurt me most, the fucking or the fact that it didn't stop there. They'd kept an emotional affair for months. Even though he said there were no feelings toward her. "She was just a fuck!" he said. "It was familiar, easy." I couldn't understand that; if it'd meant nothing, why had he still been talking with her?

"Do you love her?" I asked him.

"NO! I have absolutely no feelings for her, it was just physical!" *Physical? She looks like a dirty tramp! Is that what you like?* I was in and out of rage for days. I was angry. Angry at him for his betrayal and his disrespect, of me, our home, and everything we stood for.

I moved out. Weeks went by. I wanted nothing to do with this man. I felt like I didn't know him anymore. The man that had once been my everything felt like a complete stranger to me. I couldn't even talk to him. Emails were as much as I could handle. My heart was broken, completely broken. I wanted a divorce.

Daniel,

The more I think about it, analyze, and the more I recap, the harder it gets for me. I don't know if I can do this. I don't know if I want to keep going forward in this marriage.

Babe,

So, if you don't want to go forward you want to divorce me? Really that's what you want? I never want this and I will never do anything to hurt you again, please, forgive me. Can't you see that I live my whole life for you. I fucked up 8 months ago and everything that I have done for you and shared with you is ruined? I know that you are so hurt and angry with me, that is your right, but don't forget you are my world, my best friend, and the woman that I want to spend my whole life with. Don't throw away everything great that we have because I made a mistake. I want no one else, but you. Not now and not ever. Please give me a chance to show you the man that you married was the right one. I know that you had us on a pedestal and now that is ruined for you. I know that there is no place in the storybook fairy tale for something ugly like this. I am not perfect and I fucked up greatly. Don't throw us away because you have a set of rules. I think it would be a huge mistake if you do not let me prove my love to you. I love you so much, please don't hate me. I can't lose you. I did this because I was stupid. I actually thought that by seeing her that night I would have the power to end things with her. I did not as you know. This was the biggest mistake of my life. It took me hurting you to realize my enormous stupidity. She or no one is "that good" as you put it to cause the pain that I have caused you. You should know that one night and some emails is not worth losing a perfect wife as you. I cannot be on this earth without you, you need time to think. Tell me what you want, but I can't lose you.

    Love, me

    I sat on this for days; I hated him. I still loved him. I hated what he'd done. I wanted nothing to do with him.

    Where does one even begin to heal when your world has come crumbling down? How does one ever heal from this kind of betrayal? How do you ever get over something like this? This I had always been afraid of: betrayal and a failed marriage. I had expressed this to Danny when we first started dating. I vividly remember asking him if he'd ever cheated on anyone in his past relationships, his answer was always a no.

    "Why do you always ask me this question," he'd ask.

    "Because it says a lot about someone's character, and I rather know now than later down the line. I don't want to fall for a man who is deceitful." Once we made it "official" and became a couple, my fears intensified; I was starting to really like this guy. But what if he hurt me? One very late evening (or early morning) when I couldn't sleep, I wrote him an email expressing this fear. My email read:

    Hey babe,

    Just wanted to say hi in a different way and tell you how happy I am.

    These last few months seem almost too good to be true. You know I have fears and I'd just like to express this to you.

    I'm scared to love you, because I'm scared to lose you.

    I'm scared to be a part of your life. I'm scared to care for you because then, there won't be anything else to care for. I'm scared, because I don't want to be crazy over you.

I'm scared, but I know I want to be with you.

I'm scared to give you all my heart and soul, because you may only break it apart.

To this he replied:

Hello again babe,

I know that I just talked to you and told you that there is no reason to be scared, but let me share this with you.

I am crazy about you! I think that we both have very strong feelings for each other and similar fears. It feels great to be on the same page. It is pretty rare to find two people that feel this great about each other. You know that I am impatient and demanding and you are helping me with that just like I will help you with your fears of being hurt by continuing to show you, tell you, and express how much I care for you. You'll see!!!

The more that you "open up" and fall in love with me, the better things will become for the both of us. I promise. I realize that the usual behavior with guys is as soon as you give your heart to them, they take it for granted and end up hurting you. As long as you don't turn into crazy person this will not happen. I can't promise you the world, but I can promise you that I will always be honest, trustworthy, and the best person that I can be.

Night Night.

I can't promise you the world, but I can promise you that I will always be honest, trustworthy, and the best person that I can be. These words stayed with me. This line made me fall in love with him. This line made me believe in him. In us. In a future together. I used to remind him of these words often. They were engraved in my heart, and he had broken each and every one of these promises. He had made my worst fear come to life. He broke my heart.

Weeks went by before I could even talk to him like a real person. I had so many questions. So many doubts. So much pain inside of me, pain I didn't think I could ever recover from, pain I didn't think I could ever forgive him for. Could I ever trust him again? Could I ever see him the same way I used to? We hadn't seen each other. He emailed me daily without knowing if I would read them or not. He only hoped that I would.

Hi babe,

I wanna tell you how I feel. I just got back from the grocery store. I'm sure that you must feel super shitty because I feel extremely shitty and sad. It feels like you broke up with me or something. You are there hating me and I am here loving you and sad. You don't want to talk to me and I miss you so much. Everything that I do without you here reminds me of how it would feel like if you don't want to be with me. Going to the grocery store was always a blast with you, but today, by myself it was the most depressing thing ever. I couldn't even buy much food. The most exciting part was I got a deal on wine for you. I will bring this weekend. Even if you don't want to see me this weekend I am coming. I can drop the things that you need and go home if you want. Cleaning the house and doing laundry was also very sad. I pictured you doing it and me pinching your butt. I will do a better job at turning my socks right side out.

I cannot be on this earth without you, Love me

Hi babe,

I feel like an idiot that I put us where we are now. It sounds so pathetic of me to convince you to love me with words while my actions hurt you so deeply. I pray that you can forgive me for hurting you so terribly bad. You are the most important greatest person that I know. I am sorry I am no longer the greatest person you know. I hope to regain that title very soon.

Love, me

I wanted to see him in person. I wanted to know what I would feel and how I would feel seeing him. In person, I would be able to look in his eyes and feel either his sincerity or his lies. "We should talk," I told him. "In person."

He showed up at the door with white roses, my favorite, wine, a face full of shame, and sorrow. I could tell he hadn't slept much. There were tears in his eyes. "I'm so sorry," he said. "I never meant to hurt you; I was so stupid. I love you so much, Faby. Please, you have to forgive me."

The man I used to know was no longer the man that stood before me. The man I used to know would have never betrayed me, hurt me, broke me. I loved the man I used to know. I hated the man that had deceived me. But I also still loved the man that stood before me.

I knew the man I had fallen in love with was still in there. His heart was good. He'd made a terrible and stupid decision that would forever change our story, and I didn't know what to do or how to feel. I just stood there. Tears of sorrow, anger, pain, disappointment, and love ran down my face. *How can we ever move past this? Am I willing to move past this? Do I want to move past this?*

I still love him, this I know, but is it enough? Before I could get any words out, we embraced each other, and for a brief moment, everything felt ok.

★ ★ ★

The following few months were some of the hardest: filled with doubt, uncertainty, anger, and what remained of our love, little or big. I wanted to fight for my marriage, and at the same time, I didn't know how much fight I had in me. I was so ready to give up so many times. The anger I felt inside consumed me, but the hope that I was trying so hard to hold on to, that hope was hanging on by a thread. I'd come home, but would I stay? I wasn't sure. I didn't trust my husband. And as much as I tried, I couldn't look at him the same way. I couldn't help but question him every time he said he loved me. Every promise felt like an empty one. How could I continue if everything he said and did felt like a complete lie? There were moments I let him get close, but as soon as he touched me, all I could think was, *Is this how you touched her?* Every night while at work, I couldn't help but picture him sneaking out of the house to meet her. I mean, that's how he'd done it, on a night while I was at work late. No matter where I was or what I did, I couldn't focus. Whether alone or with him, I couldn't shake the feelings of betrayal. I wanted him, but also, I wanted him out of my life. My brain was in constant conflict with my heart. I wished he could take it all back, rewind time, and undo his fuck-up. He had broken every promise. He had broken every vow we'd made when we got married.

"You can't put conditions on love, on marriage," the priest that married us said. And one of the primary and most important questions he asked us at that time was, "Would you forgive an infidelity?" I sat on this question for a long time; it was during a pre-marriage questionnaire to figure out how compatible Danny and I were and what our ideas of marriage were. My initial ego-instinct had said no straight away, but after voicing my thoughts out loud and after considering the priest's rationale of putting conditions on love and marriage, I answered yes to this question. I would forgive. But I only said this thinking it would never happen to me, with us, in our marriage. We were solid, or so I thought. A team. Almost perfect. We'd been the envy of so many around us. Not because we tried, but because we naturally fit together. We naturally were a team. He never pulled back like the typical guy who tried to be cool and hide his feelings. Danny wasn't like that. He loved me and he showed it, always. No hidden agenda. People saw us as this "perfect couple" and I, too, had believed it. I, too, thought we were "perfect," for us. For each other. Turned out, we weren't. And that question the priest had asked us had come back to haunt me. Could I forgive infidelity? Would I forgive his infidelity?

There were moments when I thought I could forgive him. I still loved him, more than I cared to admit to myself or to him. There were moments when I felt I'd somewhat forgiven him and that we were moving forward, in the right direction. I could see him really trying to earn my trust again. I felt his sincerity, but then, anger and doubt would overtake the love. Resentment blinded me. Moments of anger came rushing in like a tsunami; I had moments where I'd lash out and fight. I screamed and threw things in his face every chance I could. Because I could. I had a right. He had fucked up, after all.

"You're an asshole who went and fucked another woman. How can I ever trust you? How can I believe your I love yous? I don't believe anything you say to me!" This went on for months. We'd have a few good days, and then, any little wrong step he took, I'd use his fuck-up to let him have it. We couldn't keep going like this. I couldn't do this any longer. I told myself that if I was going to really give this marriage another shot, I had to give it my all, otherwise, I should just walk away.

Being the fixer that I have always been, I started researching anything I could find that might help us. I read every self-help book on marriage that I came across. I read books on how to fix a broken marriage—things I never thought I'd be reading. I owned an entire collection of books I thought might help us save this marriage. Danny did his own research as a fixer himself. He reached out to an old counselor/therapist. He talked to a priest hoping he could get some insight as we had when we were in pre-marriage counseling. He talked to our much older and wiser couple friends, couples he looked up to and thought might give him advice that could help. He was desperate to heal us, to move forward, and to push himself to be the better man he knew he could be. It was in Danny's nature to want to make things better, to want to love and protect someone that had been deeply hurt. In this particular case, me, us, our marriage. As a couple of faith, we decided to make an effort together, and made an appointment to talk to the priest that had married us, hoping he might help guide us in the right direction. At our meeting with the father, we decided a couple's retreat might be good for us. It might help heal the wounds and help us move forward in our marriage. A retreat, we hoped, would open our hearts without hesitation. At the retreat, we could find each other again and discover ways to learn to trust, love without conditions, and ultimately, heal our marriage.

The drive to the retreat was quiet. We didn't have much to talk about. I didn't know what to expect of him at this retreat or if I should expect anything at all. What could possibly fix the broken trust in our marriage? Once we got there, we were separated. We weren't allowed to sleep in the same quarters. We were only allowed to see each other at specific meeting times for group discussions and partner exercises. It was actually quite nice to not be forced to be together.

At first, I was happy not being with him. But as the days went on as we worked through some of our emotions and feelings, I started to look forward to seeing each other. It almost felt like we were dating all over again. We wrote love letters to each other, and we walked, talked, and explored the grounds as we learned to speak and listen to each other again in a kind and loving way. We learned about the five languages of love: words of affirmation, quality time, gifts, acts of service, and physical touch. We learned the individual ways we expressed love, and what made us feel loved. I used to think I knew how Danny loved and felt loved, but maybe I hadn't? Maybe he hadn't really known my love language either? This was eye-opening and insightful as a young married couple. I learned Danny's primary love language was acts of service—not what I thought his would be. My primary love language is physical touch. Physical touch: the last thing I wanted at the moment was for him to touch me. Would I ever allow him to touch me again?

By the end of the retreat, I felt more connected to Danny than I had ever thought I would feel in such a short amount of time. The retreat hadn't fixed all of our problems or my doubts, but it definitely allowed me to see things—us—in a different light. Maybe there was a future for us. Maybe we could regain what we once had! Maybe our love was worth fighting for. Could we possibly come back stronger for this? I would never forget what he'd done, and I wasn't sure I would ever fully forgive, but maybe this was a step forward, a step in the right direction. Unlike how we'd arrived at the retreat, barely talking to each other, the drive home was the complete opposite. We were actually speaking, and not surface stuff either, hard, vulnerable, deep conversations. I was learning more about my husband, and he, more about me. I felt connected again for the first time in a long time, and before we knew it, we were holding hands, kissing, and making love—passionate love.

One evening, while searching on TV for a movie to watch, we came across the movie *Fireproof*, an American Christian drama film about a firefighter who, in the wake of a daring rescue of a complete stranger, realizes he has failed as a husband. In a desperate attempt to save his relationship with his wife, he embarks on a journey based on *The Love Dare*, a Christian self-help book, where he is to go on a forty-day mission to rescue his marriage from the looming specter of divorce. This film made an impact on us and kick-started the change we needed in order to move forward in our own marriage.

Without me knowing, Danny took the initiative and went all in; he bought the books and the journals and went full throttle. He embarked on *The Love Dare* journey, the forty-day challenge that would help him understand and practice unconditional love. Our marriage had been hanging on by a thread and this journey gave us hope. *The Love Dare* made him focus on himself and his heart; I began to see changes in him and in us, changes that began to mend our marriage. He put the work in day in and day out, never giving up. And before I knew it, we started to feel like the old us again. We started to fall in love with each other again, intentionally and unconditionally. *You can't put conditions on love and marriage.* We were having fun again, laughing, and connecting.

It took us a long time to recover from his infidelity, as betrayal and broken trust is not something one can easily come back from, but we put in the work and fought for our marriage. When we embarked the journey to healing our marriage, I had no idea how we would ever get past it all, or if we ever could, but I decided to give our marriage a second chance, and I am so glad that I did.

For Emma

I hope one day you can read this and know how much I love you and Dadda loved you.

After Danny's services were long over, friends and family re-turned to normal life, and the reality of my new life settled in. I began to feel extreme loneliness. I was no longer planning services like a mad woman, going to appointment after appointment keeping me moving and busy, or constantly being surrounded by people which kept my mind occupied. People had started to return to normal life which felt unfair to me. I was envious. *Why do they get to go back to normal? Why do they get to walk out of here complete while I am left broken? Why do they still have a husband and I don't? Why do their kids get to have a dad and mine doesn't?* I felt ripped off. *Why has God punished us? What did I ever do to deserve this?*

My Life was moving at a slower pace—almost in slow motion. I walked around in a fog. In denial. *Is this really my life?* During the day, sometimes my sister, neighbors, or a few of my friends still checked in on me. They came and sat, and we had wine, lots of wine. I wanted to numb the pain. I wanted to forget this was my life instead of the life I should have been living. I wanted to wake up from the nightmare and have my old life back. But nothing seemed to work. I wanted so much to glue myself back together. And I also wanted to disappear. Danny had died and some days, I wanted to die with him.

Emma kept me pretty busy being a mom, which was lifesav-ing. Had it not been for her, I probably would have lost it. Or, who knows where I'd be. Emma was three, and pretty unaware most of the time of what went on. My mom offered to stay with me for a couple months, or as long as I needed, to help with Emma, to help me, and to be my moral support, but I didn't know how to let her in. I didn't know how to let anyone in. How could anyone possibly un-derstand what I was feeling and going through?! *They can't help me, they can't fix me,* I thought. That, and I have never been one to ask for help or talk about or display my emotions. I think I unwillingly shut myself out from people. But how was I supposed to know what to do or say or how to behave when my world had just fallen apart? There is no handbook to widowhood. There are no instructions. Everyone grieves differently and this was my way; it still is sometimes. It was incredibly hard for me to let anyone into the world in my head and heart.

But as long as Emma was taken care of, I was ok. I felt better. I could breathe. Danny's parents came over daily to check in on us. They spent hours with us and then headed home. Us being together was comforting; we needed that. Danny had been the connection between us, and as long as we were together, Danny was also with us. Between Papa, Andrea, and my mom staying with me, they made sure my daughter was always happy and ok. This was incredibly helpful to me, especially on the days where I wasn't able to function and was more a zombie than a mom. Emma was my reason to get out of bed in the morning. She was the reason I functioned at all. But once night came and I put her to bed, reality would hit.

Nighttime was the worst. Everything was silent. I usually put on some white noise or jumped in the shower to cry. The shower was where I allowed myself to release. My tears would intermix with the water falling down my face and I couldn't tell which was which. I dreaded getting into bed. My empty bed. I still couldn't even look at his side of it. His empty side of the bed. I wanted so badly to feel him and his embrace. Damn it, I even missed his seldom snoring and nonstop fart wars. Everything hurt. I would have given anything to have him back. Anything. I would have gladly traded places with him. But I couldn't. And this was now my life. I lay hugging his pillow and cried myself to sleep every night—still do sometimes.

On nights when I couldn't seem to shut an eye, I walked around the house in a zombie-like state. I've never been, or even seen, a sleepwalker, but I imagine this is how it is. I walked bedroom to living room to kitchen to living room to bathroom to bedroom to upstairs to check on Emma, to make sure she was breathing, to downstairs to bedroom… I needed something to do. I needed an outlet. I needed to release some of these feelings I hadn't been able to express. So, one night I grabbed a pen and paper and with tears running down my face, I started writing.

November 19, 2015

I'm starting this journal for my little love, Emmy.

I hope one day you can read this and know how much I love you and Dadda loved you.

These are only my thoughts and memories of our love, life together, and what life without him is/has been like. I will always love you, Daniel John Ryan.

My love,

It's been over a month since you've been gone. I'm having such a hard time…

For the last month, I've been out of it. I managed to make arrangements and make things happen as far as getting you home to your resting place, but to be honest, I don't even know how I ever made that happen.

We're supposed to go on a memorial ride at Dove Springs this weekend (we leave tomorrow) and I'm having so much anxiety. I miss you so much!!!!!! The past few weeks I've tried to be so strong for you, for Emmy… I've numbed, been in denial, and tried not to cry, but the last couple days I've cried like a baby. I just miss you so much. It seems impossible that you've left me, left us. My love, I miss you so much!

I went to Ralph's today to buy some water and wine for this weekend. Emmy wanted this Dora toy so bad, so I bought it for her. In the car, I opened it for her, and then went back to Ralph's (outside) to throw out the packaging trash. When I tossed the trash, I noticed a SpaceX cup in the bin. It took me a minute for it to register that I'd seen it correctly, but there was, in fact, a SpaceX cup there. Was this a sign?

November 22, 2015

My love,

We got back from Dove Springs earlier today. It was good. Emmy had such a great time. She rode on a dirt bike for the first time. I wish you could have been here to have been the one to ride with her. Uncle Adam and Uncle Josh were amazing, though. She had the most amazing smile on her face the entire time. She is so your daughter!

Ok, so there was a moment where I swear I saw you outside of mom and dad Ryan's trailer window. Was that you?! I miss you so much, babe. Being there listening to the dirt bikes, smelling the fuel—everything reminded me of you. This was your world. Part of me feels like I don't belong. I know this world because of you. Now I feel lost… So lost.

Writing to Danny became my outlet. It was painful but comforting. I wanted to let out of my soul everything I had been holding on to. I needed so badly to talk to him, to tell him about our days and what I was feeling. I couldn't talk to anyone else the way I used to talk to him. I often talked to him in the car, or spoke out loud to the air, to the clouds. I missed my husband. I wanted to hear his voice. I yearned for his hugs, his kiss. Time kept passing by and some days just felt harder. The holidays were soon approaching and I was dreading them. How could I possibly get through them without him? He was missing so much of our lives. He was missing out on watching our baby grow. It hurt to know Emma would never have more time with her Dadda. Danny had wanted so badly to be a dad. When we found out we were having twins, he was the one who hadn't been able to keep it to himself. He wanted to shout it from the rooftops, *We are having twins!!!* He quickly made us go to his parent's house to give them the news, even though I'd been incredibly hesitant to share. I had been afraid we would share the news and like our previous pregnancies, lose my babies, but he hadn't been able to hold his excitement in. He kissed my belly over and over begging me to please share the news.

"I will love you more than yesterday!" he said.

"Sure you will," I replied as I shook my head, but ultimately agreed. How could I not? He was so excited and so cute.

After we'd lost Emma's twin and experienced all the trauma that came with Emma's birth, Danny's love and appreciation for the little life we had been gifted was more than evident. Our daughter was his pride and joy, his reason for being. Danny and I often talked about all the things we wanted to instill in her, the values we wanted to teach her, and the traumas we didn't want to pass on to her. Danny had a tumultuous childhood, as had I, and we swore we would do our best to do different by our daughter. More than anything, we couldn't wait to be parents. Danny couldn't wait to be a hands-on dad, to guide her and teach her and one day, proudly walk her down the aisle.

Emma hadn't even been walking yet when Danny already had

her sitting in the garage with him, on top of a dirt bike or playing with some of his tools. He'd been so eager to show, teach, and do with her so many of the things he had and hadn't been able to experience as a child. He talked about taking Emma by the hand and teaching her all the things he knew. *She's gonna be a little engineer one day*, he said. Sometimes, I think this too; she definitely has his engineering mind. She loves to tinker with things the way he used to. When I hear stories of Danny as a child, it's as if they are speaking of Emma, too. Danny would be so proud of her.

And now, Danny wasn't here to teach Emma how to ride a bike or help take her to school. He will never tell her what a bright kid she is and ask her how she likes her new school. He will miss out on all her milestones and the dreaded teenage years. He won't be able to give her advice the first time a boy breaks her heart, and he won't be here to walk her down the aisle the way he always dreamt he would. I grieve Danny's death as much as I grieve the future we never go to have. There are days where I feel strong and proud of myself for pushing forward, and others where I self-pity and complain to the universe how unfair all this is and ask God why I am being punished. *What have I done in a past life that I am paying for in this one?* I often ask myself. But just as I have done before, I pick myself up, pick up the broken pieces, and I keep on moving forward.

Faby Ryan

Aftermath

I want to have faith in what comes after.
I don't know what that is yet,
but I am hopeful it will be something good.

Danny's accident was the worst experience I have ever had to live through. I have woken up to nightmares, crying, hyperventilating, and unable to breathe as I relive that horrible night. And although I wasn't physically there when the accident happened and was only there for the aftermath of holding my husband's lifeless body, my brain has pieced together the event. I had enough detailed information given to me by witnesses and through the coroner's autopsy report (that I had to read through) detailing every second of those hours, painting a full picture of what occurred. What had started out as the boys last boat ride of the afternoon, turned into the worst night of my life, and everyone's worst nightmare.

Danny, an experienced and avid boater, was driving the boat. His friend, Tim, was in the passenger seat, and Danny's other friend and his two little boys, Emma's age, were in the back seat. They went downriver for about a mile and then headed back upriver about a mile and a half. They were about to make their last turn to head back to our house when they were T-boned. The other boat came out of nowhere and struck directly where Danny was sitting, launching them at least 100 yards further upriver and into the water. All passengers on our boat remained on the boat, but the entire top of the boat and engine hatch were ripped off and in the water, which is what I saw. The passengers in the back had minor injuries—cuts, scrapes—and one of the kids had to get a few staples in the back of his head. Tim suffered broken ribs and was in a lot of pain for a few weeks. I didn't see him after he was taken in the gurney at the beach. And my husband, he was instantly killed. Blunt force head and chest trauma, said the coroner's report; that was what ultimately caused my husband's death.

One decision. A last boys ride of the night, and everything changed. My and my daughter's lives were forever changed. I live with the trauma I witnessed that night. I can hear myself screaming Danny's name, asking him to wake up, both of us covered in his blood. I replay this scene over and over in my head hoping to wake up, hoping to change the outcome, but there is nothing I can do to change it. And there is nothing I can do to make it go away.

People like to say everything happens for a reason, but I see no reason why this happened to us. I see no reason why I was left a thirty-two-year-old widow with a three-year-old special needs child who had already suffered enough. After Danny's death, I lost all of my faith. I couldn't understand why God would make us suffer this way or what I had done to deserve this. I have blamed myself. *I should have been there. Maybe I could have saved him.* And in those moments of doubt, I've had to remind myself it wasn't my fault. I've questioned my life. I've questioned my purpose. I had not only lost my husband, I had also lost a future. Most people in our lives only see a fraction of our loss. They only see our primary loss, my husband, but there are so many secondary losses people don't see: identity, intimacy, security, partnership, a support system, dreams for a future, a parenting partner, and so much more. In losing Danny, I also lost myself. I was changed on a cellular level, and from that there is no going back. One day at a time, I have regained faith. Faith in something greater than me. Faith in myself. Faith in a future. Faith in what comes after. I wake up each morning and try and find purpose.

Five

*A year of new challenges, new goals, living with intention,
and looking forward to what came next.*

Five. "When Emma turns five, I am going to throw her the most amazing *Cinco de Mayo* themed birthday party," I said to Danny as we sat in the Pediatric Intensive Care Unit at Children's Memorial in Long Beach. Two months after coming home from the NICU, after a visit to one of her gastroenterologists where he'd made a huge medical mistake with her feeding tube (MIC-KEY button placement) that almost cost us her life, Emma was transferred from Little Co of Mary Hospital in Torrance and admitted to Children's Hospital in Long Beach. Emma underwent an emergency surgery where they had to cut her open across her entire stomach to flush her insides before she went septic. Because of Emma's history and fragile state, the NICU readmitted her for a night while she was being transferred to the PICU, which the hospital didn't provide. This was one of the scariest experiences a parent could ever go through, especially after barely having survived the NICU. Our baby was fighting for her life yet again. This was late December, which meant we would be spending the holidays in the hospital. Danny and I didn't want to leave Emma for a second, so for the next few weeks, we were staying at the Ronald McDonald House across from the hospital.

We were so scared for Emma's life and the uncertainty of what came next that I'd needed to hope for the future. I needed something to look forward to. I knew my daughter was a fighter and she'd survive yet again, but my mind was going crazy. I needed a distraction, and looking forward to a future, making a plan, gave me hope. "I am going to hire a mariachi and a taco guy and bring all the drinks and candy from Mexico. I'm going to decorate with the most vibrant colors, and I'm going to…" Danny just listened. He was used to my big party planning ideas, and although five felt unattainable, I felt hopeful. I wanted to plan ahead. I wanted to see a future—a future where my baby girl would have a future.

Getting us to five became my goal. Something to look forward to. My happy place. The big milestone. And the happy little event planner in me had years to plan the biggest party we would ever have. Danny shook his head, rolled his eyes, and smiled away. He knew this would be a whole "Faby Production" and nothing would make me change my mind.

"Ok, my little planner, let's make it happen. Our little family deserves it, and you know I love me some tacos!"

A few months before Emma's fifth birthday, I recalled this conversation. Emma's fifth birthday loomed over me. I couldn't possibly throw this birthday party now. Not without Danny. This had been our plan. Our Party. Our milestone. It would never be the same without him. The closer Emma got to five, the more my grief intensified. I was angry that Danny wouldn't get to be a part of this huge milestone in our daughter's life. I was angry I would have to do this on my own. I was sad for Emma, even though she had no idea. She didn't know how much this birthday meant to me and her daddy. When she'd been born, with all odds against her, we weren't sure we'd even make it to year one, and here I was now, with an almost-five-year-old.

One morning, after much processed grief, I woke up with a new mindset, "Screw it! I'm having Emma's party, not only for her but for Danny, and me, too!" We deserved to celebrate this amazing milestone; Danny would have wanted it. So, I went into crazy party planning mode. I could see Danny shaking his head, rolling his eyes, and smiling away. I spent months planning every single detail, just the way I had envisioned it that night in the PICU. I made invitations. I booked the mariachi. I spent endless nights crafting every single thing on my Pinterest board. I even booked the taco guy Danny had always loved. The candy and tequila, straight from Mexico it would come. I was excited. Hopeful. I knew Danny would be there with us the entire way.

When the day of the party finally arrived, I felt a sense of accomplishment, not only for having put together a party but also, for making it to five. Emma reached this amazing milestone that had once seemed so far away. I was proud of us for making it to five on our own. For having come this far. The last two years were some of the most incredibly trying times in our life, but we somehow made it to this day. I was a young widow and solo mommy to our most precious miracle, my five-year-old. We did it. We survived. And this celebration would be for all of us. For the pain and the joys and the hope that had carried us through. For our loss, but also, for the love that would forever remain.

The party was put together beautifully. Colorful streamers, banners, and giant paper flowers filled my entire backyard. Tall pub tables were arranged and draped in shades of hot pink, teal, yellow, and red. *Serapes* draped the main tables filled with arrays of Mexican candies and a beautiful two-tiered cake adorned with giant eatable flowers. I even purchased an original Mexican wooden bar just for the occasion. Danny would have thought I was completely crazy, but he would have loved the assortment of tequila, *cantaritos*, and beer I displayed.

We were surrounded by about eighty of our dear family and friends, all dressed in traditional Mexican outfits, the birthday girl being the cutest one. I set up craft stations for the kids where they painted maracas to take home as souvenirs. Kids, along with grownups, jumped in the giant inflatable jumper until they exhausted themselves. Emma was happy. Mommy was, too. We broke a giant piñata filled with candies and treats that my Aunt Rosy and Uncle More had brought Emma from Mexico. The mariachi came in at the perfect time to sing to the birthday girl Las Mañanitas, the traditional Mexican birthday song. I even ended up singing two songs with the mariachi—I couldn't help myself. If you know me, you know how much I love mariachi! We sang, danced, and partied the night away. It was a kid's party as well as a grown-up party. It could not have been more perfect, except for one thing: I missed Danny with all of my heart. I wished he could have been there. I wished he could have seen it all come together, and although not physically, I know he was there with us. I could feel his presence in the air. *We made it to Five, my love. You should see her; she is just amazing!*

Emma turning five changed a lot of things for me. It opened my eyes to new, bigger possibilities. Just like we had when Emma was three and had her gastrostomy tube removed, I felt hopeful again. I wanted to live. I wanted to explore. I wanted to show Emma there was more to life than what we had experienced and lived so far. I wanted to show Emma the world. I wanted to show me the world. I wanted to live for Danny, for the life that was robbed from him. For the life we had envisioned. I wanted to look forward toward a brighter future for me and Emma. It was us against the world, and I wanted to show the world, and myself, we could do this; we would make it.

Five would be a big year for us Ryan girls. At the end of this same month, May 2017, we took our very first solo trip to the beautiful beaches of Mexico: Cabo San Lucas and La Paz. I was a little scared, I'm not going to lie. Traveling alone to another country with a five-year-old was a brave move. I never thought I'd have the courage to do things like book a flight on a whim to another country, but I was on a mission. I would not allow fear to overtake my life. It would be scary and different, absolutely, but if I had survived Emma coming into this world the way she had and my husband dying, I could survive anything. Emma was incredibly excited for this trip. She packed her pink Minnie Mouse luggage with her favorite swimsuits and toys and on we went. And just like she had on our first trip to Disney World, she carried her daddy's photo with her. "I want Daddy with us," she said.

The trip started off a little rocky, and for a moment there, we weren't sure we would be able to make it. First, we missed our original flight and had to take a later one, which screwed up our itinerary. Then, on our way from the airport to La Paz, we got into a gnarly car accident. Our flight had gotten in very late and it was pitch-black on the road. We were on a toll road and it seemed pretty safe, similar to our freeways in California, except it wasn't. A crazy cow came out of nowhere and we hit it. Hard. I was scared for my life and my daughter's life. Emma had fallen asleep on the drive. When the car came to a stop, I hit the windshield and was bleeding from my head and hands. I quickly called for Emma, unbuckled myself, and when I turned back, she was still fast asleep, holding Daddy's picture in her hands. There were pieces of broken glass all over, so I panicked and quickly got to her and checked to make sure she wasn't hurt anywhere. There was not one scratch on her. I said a silent prayer and thanked Danny for keeping our baby safe. I knew he'd had a hand in it.

Minutes later, a car pulled up to help us. It was a family who had seen the crash; they helped clean my cuts and tried to get as much glass off of me as they could. Soon after, an ambulance arrived and we were taken to a private hospital in town. We spent the night in the hospital, our first night in Mexico. The lady who helped us the night before, an angel in disguise, had promised to come back for us, and she kept her promise. She picked us up at the hospital in the morning, drove us to get medications, and then took us to our hotel. I will forever be grateful to her and her family; they were heaven-sent in a time we needed them most. We were able to rest for a little back in our room. I was in less pain except for my hands, but I decided I wouldn't let this ruin our trip. I was in survival mode.

We went on to spend some beautiful days exploring and sunbathing on the turquoise beaches of La Paz. We went spearfishing on a panga and tried snorkeling for the first time. It was unlike anything I had ever experienced. Emma discovered a newfound love for horses, which we rode on the beach multiple times. We ate some of the yummiest food, and Emma even made a friend on the playground at the beach; they barely understood each other as one spoke only English and the other only Spanish, but they made it work and had a wonderful time. La Paz turned out to be an incredibly magical place, one I wish to visit again for sure. Our first Mommy and me trip would definitely not be the last.

The big Five, would go on to be just that, big! In September of this same year, we traveled to Greece! Greece, number one on my bucket list ever since I was a kid. I know this sounds crazy, a huge birthday party and two international trips in one year, but it was like I was making up for lost time. Our experience in Mexico had reinvigorated my desire for living. I wanted to feel alive. I needed to feel alive. I wanted to experience life outside of everything I had known and had been through the last two years. In hindsight, I was also running away from my life at home and everything that reminded me of my loss and my grief, so if I had any opportunity to travel the world, escape it all and watch my daughter as she explored and lived life, I would most definitely jump on it.

Greece was unlike any other place I had ever been to. Our first stop, the capital of Greece, Athens, was surreal. The day we arrived, we checked in to our cute little Grecian courtyard apartment with the most stunning green door. That same night, we got to visit the Parthenon on the Acropolis at sunset, which is an experience in itself. There were lots of tourists, even though it was the off-season, but it was still amazing. In the two days we were there, we visited the Par-

liament and experienced the Changing of the Guard. We visited the
National Archeology Museum and Monastiraki Square. We shopped
in the Plaka, ate some of the most delicious gyros—lots and lots of
gyros—and drank endless espresso as we walked the streets of Athens. We visited temples and ruins just like I'd read about in the books
when I was a kid not much older than Emma. This was a dream, and I
wanted to soak it all in with my little peanut.

After Athens, we jumped on a ferry and made it to the island
of Naxos, the largest of the Cyclades, and by far one of my favorite
Islands. In Naxos, we traveled amazing landscapes by buggies along
the mountain villages, ancient ruins, and stretches along the beach.
We ate at the most delicious home-style restaurants and drank some
delicious Ouzo. After a couple days in Naxos, we jumped back on the
ferry on to our next destination: Thera, commonly known as Santorini, Greece. I don't think I really have to say this, but Santorini was a
dream! It was what I envisioned and more. The white buildings with
blue dome rooftops overlooking the Aegean Sea were stunning to say
the least.

We walked the cobbled streets of Fira and Oia as we ate and
shopped and snapped photo after photo hoping this would freeze
these moments that would live with us forever. We went and experienced wine tasting in Santorini as we overlooked the incredible
endless blue sea. Emma rode a donkey on the steep hills in Oia and
swam naked in the black lava beach; she definitely took it all in. My
baby was happy, experiencing the time of her life and so was Mommy.
We even brought home souvenir necklaces with our names written in
Greek.

And last but not least, we ended our trip visiting the wonderful island of Chania, Crete, Greece. We started in Heraklion; toured
Rethymno to Elafonisi beach, which was a dream; and visited one of
the most amazing monasteries, sitting on a cliff overlooking the ocean.
Although we got to see a lot, Crete is definitely a place where you
need more time to explore. We were running out of time and had
to get back to Athens to prepare for our next stop in Madrid, Spain,
and then home. We didn't get to spend as much time in Madrid as we
would have liked to, as it was a quick trip before coming home, but it
is definitely on the *Go Back To* list!

As you can see, we were ending Five with a bang, and there was more where that came from. In December we—I—decided to book a quick trip to Siesta Key, Florida, over the ending holidays. We left Christmas day and spent New Year's Eve in a new place, different, not home. We explored the white sand beaches of Siesta Key and immersed ourselves in the incredible sunsets that painted the sky with every hue of gold, pink, purple, and blue. The never-ending sunsets allowed us to build a snowman with the powdery white sand, as if it were snow. On New Year's Eve, we went out to an early dinner and then came back to the house we were staying in. It was calm and quiet, nothing crazy. All in all, Florida had been very welcoming to us. It was just what we'd needed at the time.

2017 was a year of new challenges, new goals, living with intention and trying new things, and looking forward to what came next.

#ShowingEmmyTheWorld

Oh, the places you will go.

In March of 2018, I turned thirty-five, halfway between thirty and forty. To celebrate such a milestone, I wanted to travel and keep showing Emma and myself the world. So, I took Emma on a weeklong trip to Costa Rica, *Pura Vida*. We were very much looking forward to getting away and enjoying some good times sunbathing on the beach, taking in different cultures, hopefully hiking some waterfalls, and maybe seeing and adventuring in some of the famous volcanos. We didn't really know what to expect as we'd never traveled to that part of the world before, but all the stuff we saw online displayed some amazing adventures; Emma was really looking forward to seeing some monkeys and going swimming.

We landed in Costa Rica four days before my birthday. It could not have been more perfect; we would have time to enjoy this amazing place before and through my actual birthday. For the first part of our trip, we would be staying in Guanacaste at the Four Seasons resort at Peninsula Papagayo. The night we arrived, we weren't able to get a good view of the resort as it was late and dark, but upon awakening, we woke up to one of the most beautiful places. The private house we were staying at (thanks to a friend's generosity) was on the beachfront with the most stunning view of the Pacific Ocean.

We decided to get the day started early so we could soak up as much as we could for the time we'd be staying. We went and explored the grounds, and with the beach being a short walking distance away, I decided to go for a run along the waterfront and soak in some of the salty air, the perfect way to start the day. Later, Emma and I explored some of the pools and also checked out the kid's club the resort provided. It was one of the coolest kid's clubs I had ever seen, with an itinerary of activities throughout the day that kept the kids learning and entertained, and a private, gated, kids pool, fully staffed with its own lifeguard and crew members. I knew Emma would definitely enjoy this place and I felt comfortable knowing she was being watched and taken care of very well.

The week was off to a great start! The next three days were spent swimming, sunbathing, and drinking coconuts on the beach while Emma played with Crabby, her new pet crab. We toured some of the surrounding areas where the locals lived and found some other incredible beaches and ridiculously yummy food. We hiked through the surrounding areas of the resort and found ourselves at Andaz beach, one of the coolest beaches, unlike anything I had ever seen. It was like being in the middle of the woods and at the beach all at the same time. Our walking adventures lead us to some pretty cool educational tours where they spoke about the animals and wildlife of the area. On one of the days, Emma played in the kid's club and met new friends as Mommy rented a Jet Ski and went on a day's adventure exploring the surrounding waters. I have to give it to my little adventurer. She is always up for anything and can go with the flow very easily.

Four days into our trip, we left Guanacaste and traveled to Rincón de la Vieja, where we stayed at a really cool hotel, Hacienda Guachipelín, a farm to table, cows, chickens, and horses type of place. It was the complete opposite of what the previous days of our trip had been like, but I wanted us to experience what true, authentic Costa Rica was like. We had the time of our lives there. We rode horses and hiked to the most stunning waterfalls where we swam in the clearest of waters in areas where you never thought such waterfalls existed. We explored mud pots where we indulged in sacred muds and hot springs. And we saw some of the most incredible rainbows, no rain needed. The restaurant at the Hacienda had some of the most delicious food I have ever eaten—we couldn't get enough. Emma got to play the marimba with the coolest guy there, and she milked cows to get a taste of what farm life was like. I'm not sure if she did the work or if the guy helping did most of it, though. All in all, my baby was having the most incredible time. Toward the end of our trip, we explored the national park, Volcán Rincón del la Vieja, and got to see an active volcano. It was incredible. And then it was time to head home. My birthday Costa Rica trip with my princess had been a success. Being with her was all that mattered and although no trip is perfect with kids, this kid was definitely starting to be a world traveler!

In April of that same year, I decided to go on a healing solo trip and hike Havasupai, an Indian reservation deep in the Grand Canyon.

As much as I wanted to take Emma, she just would not have been able to take on such a tough escapade. I was going through a very difficult time and wanted to take this time to be on my own for a few days and do some much needed soul searching and healing. Nothing like nature to provide this. I was in desperate need and though this trip wouldn't fix the pain I was suffering, being in nature couldn't possibly hurt. The trip would not be easy, but it was a challenge I was willing and determined to take on.

The very difficult desert hike to Havasupai is a ten-mile hike deep in the Grand Canyon and ten miles back out. Havasupai is not part of the Grand Canyon National Park, though, it is part of the Indian reservation and requires a permit which one must purchase in advance to be able to enter the area. In recent years, Havasu Falls has become an incredibly famous area, and it is very difficult to obtain permits, which must be done months in advance because they usually sell out within the hour. Lucky for me, I'd been able to get my hands on one. The hike into Havasu Falls is very rocky, sandy, and has very little shade, so one must prepare, I read.

I had done the research, prepared, and was in great physical condition to take on the hike, but nothing prepared me for what I was about to experience. I started the hike early morning, right after sunrise at about 6 am. The views were breathtaking and stunning. I couldn't believe my eyes. I was already in love. The hike started off easy, but the more I hiked down, the harder it got. I went at a pretty good pace, not rushing myself at all. The first mile of the trail switchbacks back and forth down into the canyon—not too bad. The next three miles were mostly in the sun and it definitely intensified the hike. I was hydrated and had sun protection, but I felt it nonetheless. The rest of the way into the village of Supai was shady and made the hike a little easier; I was also starting to get even better views as I hiked along the creek. From the village, it would take about another mile to get to the campground, with Havasu Falls just a short distance away. All in all, the hike in took about six hours, including stopping to rest and eat. I was not in a rush.

As I walked around the corner and got my first sight of Havasu Falls, I could not believe what my eyes were seeing: the most incredible, breathtaking, blue, teal, bright water I had ever seen in my life.

I had to stop and ask someone to please take my photo. I wanted to keep this moment forever. As I continued into the campground and through the falls, I was mesmerized by the stunning waters and incredible views. If you don't know or have never seen what these falls look like, please, do me a favor and look them up.

The hike was long and I was pretty exhausted, so with help, I set up camp, and relaxed for a while. I had a perfect front row seat to one of the most incredible places in the world and I was going to take it all in during the next couple of days. That evening ended with a slumber under the star-studded sky. It was perfection. The following bright new day started with coffee while overlooking the next set of falls, Mooney Falls. It was a continuation of breathtaking scenery, like a painting that was never ending. Pure magic. I barely had time to think of anything else with these views; my heart was content.

The hike down to Mooney Falls was quite the adventure. I had to hike down sketchy, slippery, muddy stairs and a rope and chain-link ladder for I cannot tell you how many feet—I tried not to think about it. But once I was at the bottom of the falls, it was all worth it. Mooney Falls led to another four-mile hike along the river into Beaver Falls, another breathtaking waterfall which had one of the most incredible blue, tiered pools. I think Beaver Falls was probably my favorite. It was wide, extra blue, and endless. At the end of the tiered pools, the end of Beaver Falls, was a waterfall that kept calling my name. I stood at the top of the falls and without thinking twice, I decided I wanted to jump. Don't ask me what came over me. Part of me wanted to take it all in, literally and figuratively, and part of me, the me with all these fears I had been carrying over the last three years wanted to let go and feel free for a moment. Jumping into those falls was letting go of my fears. Feeling a rush of adrenaline run through my body was my way of feeling alive again. So, I jumped. It was the most freeing and liberating thing I had ever done.

The three days, two nights in Havasupai had been just what I needed. For the time I was there, I felt free. I gave up on the shit that was hurting me, and although I never voiced it, inside, I knew that trip was the end of so much of my grief and the beginning of something new. It took me a while to realize this, but slowly, I was beginning to peel back layers of myself, layers I had fought so hard not to pay attention to. And I was learning to let go of some of my pain.

Havasupai opened up an even bigger love for travel and exploring the world, for exploring things and places I had always envisioned but had been too afraid to. I wanted more than ever to take life by the horns and share with Emma a whole new world of possibilities. Traveling started out as an escape from my world and the reality of my new life, but it became healing, and I would take any and all opportunities that came my way to do just that.

In June of that year, we traveled to Loveland, Colorado, where we were part of our good friend's wedding, Emma was the perfect flower girl. Of course, we had to take advantage of the trip, so we took a few days to explore the beautiful state and some of its incredible National Parks. At the wedding, we met the most incredible people whom we quickly made friends with. Emma and I like to make friends everywhere we go (we are not shy people). And by the Fourth of July, we were vacationing with our new friends in Chicago, their hometown. I fell in love with Chicago and all of its beautiful spots—Millennium Park, the famous bean, and the river, to name a few. Chicago is one place that I would definitely like to go back to.

Chicago was followed by Mexico, on a family trip. Then Sedona, on a hiking adventure. And in August, during Emma's summer break, I took her on a California road trip from Mammoth Lakes to Reno, NV, to Lake Tahoe through Sonoma on a hot air balloon ride to Stinson Beach. Then, we went through San Francisco to Monterrey, then Paso Robles, Santa Barbara, and all along the coast until we made it back home again. We had one of the most amazing summers, bonding, arguing, pouting, and getting irritated with each other, but together. #ShowingEmmytheWorld for me is not just about spoiling my daughter with trips and things; it is about this time together we will never get back.

People often ask me how I could have put my five-year-old on a fifteen-hour flight to Europe, or how can I travel with a kid all the time? "Isn't it exhausting?" I hear often. "I don't know how you do it. I dread traveling with kids." Or, they want to wait until the kids are older and are able to behave more. I will tell you this: I don't have any other choice. If I want to travel, my daughter comes with me. But more than that, I wouldn't want it any other way. I don't want to look through photos of my travels one day only to discover the one person who means more than the world to me wasn't with me. My advice is don't wait. Show your babies the world. I promise, you won't regret it. I know I never have.

Heaven

Maybe when we lose someone, they are not far at all,
just a few inches away.

I search for signs everywhere. I want to believe Danny is up in heaven watching over Emma and me, making sure we are ok, wiping my tears away, and guiding Emma along the way. I know Danny would never abandon us. More often than not, he sends me signs: Monarch butterflies, usually in twos. Rainbows, when there is no rain. Feathers, when there are no birds around. Pennies from heaven, although I always get dimes. He sends me songs on the radio when I need them most, and serenades Emma and me with "Don't Stop Believin', his favorite song, so we know it's him. I've seen lights flicker and turn on, on their own, and I have heard the doorbell ring when no one is there. But my favorite one is when he visits me in my dreams. One dream in particular I had a about nine months after he passed. An incredibly vivid dream—more than a dream—it felt like a visitation. When I woke, I quickly wrote it in my dream journal so I wouldn't forget a detail.

July 25, 2016
I saw Danny in my dream today...
I am at a party with friends: high school friends, friends I haven't seen in years, and friends I have now. I'm sitting by the pool telling my friends how much I am hurting, how my brain has blocked me of my memories, how much I can't remember Danny. I can't remember the good times, our memories together, his voice... Suddenly I feel someone come up from behind me. "Hi," the voice says. It's Danny's voice. He holds me from behind and says, "Hi, babe!" I turn around and it is him. His old self, messy hair, shorts and a shirt, and his rainbow chanclas (sandals). I hug and hold him tight, then start crying on his chest. I don't say a word, I can't, they won't come out. I just sob on his chest, nonstop. There is so much I want to say to him. There is so much I want to ask him, but the words won't come out. He then tells me, "It's going to be ok; you're going to be ok!" Then disappears. I sit there crying. There was so much I wanted to say.

I woke up sobbing. It had all been so real. I know he was there, not like in a normal dream. This was so much more. This dream is what keeps me going sometimes when I feel like I can't. I hold on to his words: *"It's going to be ok; you're going to be ok!"*

Emma has had dreams, too. She has felt him. When she was smaller, we would find her alone in her toy room laughing and talking as if she was playing with someone. There were nights when I'd check in on her in the middle of the night only to find her talking to someone. I would ask her and all she could talk about was Dadda. *Mommy, remember when Dadda used to play with me in the pool? Momma, remember when Dadda took me to SpaceX.* I want to believe it was Danny, talking with her and sharing those memories of them together so she wouldn't forget him. I've read that because of their innocence, children are often visited by spirits of loved ones. And I believe with all of my heart that Danny has never left her. He is always around. I recently read a story from another widow that went like this:

When a baby is being created in the womb, it thinks it's alone because it can't see anyone. It doesn't know how close it is to its mother. It can hear and sense things and presences, but everything feels far away. But in reality, it's just a few inches away. The baby is right there with its mom. It just can't see that. But the mother knows. The mother is carrying the baby the whole time and doing everything she can to care for it and protect it. -Amanda Kloots

Maybe when we lose someone, they are like a growing baby: just a few inches away. There are days I can feel Danny. I can sense his energy. Just a few inches away. I imagine Danny talking to Emma every night. I imagine she asks him about his life in heaven with Ethan, her twin, as she does me. *Dadda, what does Ethan look like? Does he like school like I do? What do you guys play? Do you think he would like me?* I imagine her catching him up on her days at school, telling him about her little crush. Him laughing it off but nervous to see his little girl growing up so fast. I imagine they laugh and play until she tires out for the night.

When I think of Danny in heaven, I picture a beautiful place with colors unlike anything I've ever seen before. An array of all my favorite flowers where the seasons don't play a role: white, red, and pink roses; white, pink, and lavender hydrangeas; yellow and red tulips; Cymbidiums and other orchids in every color; and many, many more brightly painted flowers lining acres and acres of green hills. There are butterflies of every color flying in every which way, rainbows painting the sky without the need for rain. Deep in between the hills, a huge waterfall leading to a lagoon where Danny and Ethan like to play with RC boats. One of the things Danny loved about our river house was the lagoon, where he would spend endless hours tinkering with his toy boats. I can see him now, showing our son how they work. I can see both Ethan and Danny handpicking the heavenly sign they will send for the day—the monarch, the dimes, the feathers.

When I picture my son, I picture a boy version of Emma, with the same big personality, full of life, an eagerness to learn, and a huge sense of humor, just like Daddy. Ethan is a little taller than Emma but has the same small frame. He has blonde hair like Danny used to have when he was little, but with curls like mine. He has bright blue eyes, just like his Papa and his great-grandmother, whom he's probably already met. Ethan is kind and tender, although on the outside, he likes to play tough, just like me. He has a giving soul, which he gets from both Danny and me. When Emma talks about Ethan, this is how she sees him too; this is how she's described him after he's visited her dreams. "Mommy, I think Ethan really likes math, like me."

"You think so?" I asked.

"He's very smart, Mommy!" This love for math both Emma and Ethan get from me. Danny was never a math-loving guy—pretty ironic because he was an engineer and worked with math a lot. He was naturally very smart. I, on the other hand, have always had a love for math.

Maybe Ethan, like Emma, is a perfect mixture of both Danny and me. And I hope that Ethan, too, asks Danny about me. *Daddy, what was Mommy like?* I know he does. The love we shared while he was in my womb has never gone away. I hope he knows this. I hope he knows how much his sister and I love him.

The love Danny had, and continues to have, for Emma and me he now gets to share with our son. And it fills my heart to know Ethan is no longer alone. Although I wish with all of my heart we could all be together here on earth, I know we will reunite one day.

For now, I picture them on outings talking about how much they love and miss us. I imagine them planning the next adventure. Exploring the hills on a beautifully sunny day, sun hitting their faces as they mountain bike through them. I see Danny tinkering in the garage, showing Ethan how the bike works and what he should and shouldn't do. "Come here, Ethan, let me show you," I can hear him say, "You're gonna love this!" And some days, I can see them out on the water, cruising downriver on a boat, wishing Emma and I were with them, as much as we wish we were there, too.

For now, they have each other, and every other one of the loved ones we have lost. I know they get to see and spend time with them, too. I bet they surround them with so much love. My Mami Celia and Grandma Vi have definitely been very present; their nurturing ways and loving hearts could never keep them away. I bet they get along so well, too. My cousin Mickey, and Danny's nephew, Bailey— they've probably had a good game of soccer by now, something they both loved and had in common. I know there is a big happy family up there in heaven, just waiting for us to join the party. In the meantime, they watch over us; they make sure we are safe, and more often than not, they send us signs that they are with us.

Earth

To my forever love

Dear Danny,

*   I sit here on the day of your sixth-year death anniversary, my toes submerged in the cold wet sand as I stare out into the still water; the colors are changing from night to day as the sun is about to rise. Beautiful shades of gold, pink, and purple glisten in the river, the very same river where I last saw you. I don't remember it being this calm, this peaceful, this serene. The water seems different than it was that night when everything moved so quickly. I wanted to come here today, alone, for the first time in six years and allow myself a moment with you, just you. I've been so scared of this moment; I didn't want you to see me cry. I've tried so hard to stay strong, but some days, like today, it is just too hard. It has taken me six years to find the courage to get here, but as I allow the tears to flow, I know I am allowing myself to heal in the process. I miss you so much, my love. I wish so much you were here. As life with its synchronicities would have it, today, on the sixth-year anniversary of your death, I write the last chapter to my book, but not the end to my story.*

*   As for us, Emma and me, we try so much to live a life with purpose. After you went on to heaven, my love, I made a promise to live life to its fullest. Not as the cliché many use but as we define it. For us, living life to the fullest means living a life you never had the opportunity to live. Your life was cut short. And I've had to learn to pick up the pieces. I've had to glue myself and our life back together, piece by piece. It has been the hardest thing I've ever had to do. There are days I don't know if I can go on, but just when I want to give up, your smiling face pops into my head. "You've got this, my love," I can hear you say. And I gather strength from somewhere deep within me and I carry on.*

Emma is now a thriving, energetic, full of life nine-year-old. She's not our little girl anymore, and she makes sure to let me know this daily! Can you believe she's in fourth grade now? Time has sure traveled fast; although some days, life seems to move way too slow, especially on the really hard days. We keep a pretty busy schedule filled with school, homework, therapies, and Emma's newfound love for dance and art. She is taking violin lessons at school, which she loves, along with ballet, jazz, and hip-hop at a dance center; I've become a dance mom and I love it. I am so proud of her. You should see her babe; she definitely gets her dance moves from me, no offense.

It has been incredible watching her turn into this amazing little human being. She has so much personality and love for life, and so much to offer this world. But at the same time, she also knows too much. She's experienced more in her nine years of life than any child should ever have to. Her grief is her own and she deals the best she knows how to, but sometimes it is a lot. There have been nights where I've embraced her as she is falling apart and the tears are nonstop—nothing I can do to make her longing and pain go away. I have felt helpless.

She has a hard time expressing her grief and sometimes without realizing, she says things that break my heart. Like when she wished me dead only so you can come for a while and take my place. "Then you can switch back," she said. Or she'll ask me to call heaven so she can hear your voice and speak to you "for just a minute." "Please, mommy," she begs. She misses you so much. We miss you so much. She has been through grief therapy and that helped at the time, but grief has its way of sneaking up on her, especially at school where she takes extra notice of her friends with their dads or when school activities call for a dad's day. I've found myself aching for her at family functions when everyone's families are complete except for ours. Our daughter is resilient and strong, but some days she tires out, she shuts down, and she can only express through attitude.

I wish I could take some of her pain away. When she struggles, I remember the words you said to her one day in the NICU as you watched her being resuscitated and struggling to breath: "You have to pull through, my little love, you just have to. I can't do this for you; I'm sorry but you have to do this one all on your own. I'm right here. I love you. Mommy loves you." And I watched you place your hand over her, loving her, protecting her. You knew just what to say and do. I strive to have the right words. To do right by her. To be her support when she needs me most. She is the light in my life. I wish you could be here to experience how incredible she is. She gives me life. She shines brighter than the sun. She is so much like you. And every day she looks more and more like you, too!

The last six years have been trial and error for me. Trying to figure out what works and what doesn't. How to grieve. How to keep going. How to not get stuck. How to not lose myself in the process. Picking up the pieces as a solo-everything has been hard—harder than I ever thought. I have cried in desperation asking God "Why?" searching for reasons and answers. I have found myself alone, more alone than not. I have grieved other losses as much I have grieved losing you. And I have also realized who is there and who isn't. Not only for me but mostly for our daughter. When it comes to Emma, everything hurts. You know this. We went through it when Emma was born: feeling lost, alone, and abandoned. Remember after months in the NICU when you had to call out a few people for not being there for you while our daughter was dying? Yeah, I've had those same feelings. I have lost many people along this journey of losing you, but I have also had a little tribe of people rooting for me. Rooting for us. Cheering Emma and me along the way as they bear witness to my struggles and triumphs.

I have tried to live a life you would be proud of. I hope I have made you proud. I have made it a purpose to keep your memory alive. To include you in all we do. Your name, your photo, the incredible husband and father you always were is very present in our daily lives. If it's not me telling a Daddy story, it is Emma. We can't go to a pool or the river without her saying, "Mommy, can you twirl me like Daddy used to do?!" She was so little when you left us, but she remembers you so clearly. I hope that in me writing our story, as she gets older and understands more, she gets to know more of you. Not only the incredible dad you were to her as she remembers you but more of you, the man. I have tried not to put you on a pedestal, as there is no such thing as perfect. I have tried to keep your memory alive and as real as possible without romanticizing our story or who you were. Our story was not perfect. You were not perfect. We made mistakes like most humans, but as I write and teach my daughter about the man who was her father, I also want her to know how, like all human beings, Daddy had good days and bad days. Daddy was incredible, but he also had his flaws and weak moments, just like Mommy. I don't ever want her idealizing an unattainable perfect as she strives to be more like you or me. I want her to know we all fall down at times, but it is in how we get back up that truly matters.

And back up is where I am heading. Where I strive to take us. I try and find joy in the little things. Especially in Emma's smiles. She brings so much life into my world and I know as I watch her, you live inside of her. Her gleaming eyes, bright smile, and kind heart—it is all you and me and the love with which we lived our lives together, that love that created such a beautiful human. The last six years I have dedicated to growing as a person and as a mother, to finding peace within the pain, healing my trauma, and finding my purpose. I can't say I am fully there yet, but I can say I am sure as hell on my way.

I want to show Emma there is so much more to this world than what we've known it to be so far. We tend to spend so much time worrying about tomorrow that sometimes, we forget the now, today, our present. I don't know what tomorrow will bring, but I know I don't want to live in fear any longer.

I want to live. I want to keep showing Emma the world. Did I tell you I even started a hashtag a year after you died? I sure did. In honor of you, I made #ShowingEmmyTheWorld because you and I never got to. We have traveled to many astounding places—more places than I ever thought I would get to see—and I promise you there will be more. The other night we were looking through your passport and Emma said, "Wait, Daddy went to London and Japan and....?" He sure did! So, it is on our list to travel to all the places stamped on Daddy's passport, you just wait and see.

There is no antidote to loss, pain, or grief, but joy and grief can live side by side as they are forever intertwined. I am determined to live a full life. A life of happiness. We deserve happiness. I now know I am worthy. I know there will continue to be hard days, moments, weeks, and months, but I will strive every day to live a life of joy while I heal my pain. And though I don't have all the answers yet, I am on a forever search.

Love you forever,

Your wifey

Acknowledgements

It takes a village to put a book together, and that is what I've had.

First and foremost, thank you, Davina Ferreira, for believing in me and my story. Your encouragement, guidance, and weekly, sometimes daily inspiration helped me get through the process of writing this book. Thank you to my Alegria Familia, my classmates, who sat with me weekly as I shared, cried, and healed. Thank you for the laughs, the tears, and the journey. Thank you, Ernesto Olivares, for shooting the cover of my book and for once more being a part of my journey. Thank you, Sabrina Butler, my amazing editor and proofreader, I couldn't have done this without you. Your incredible hard work, love for your art, and dedication made this possible. To Carlos Mendoza, my book designer, it was a pleasure working with you; your work is incredible! It really does take a village!

Thank you to my daughter, Emma, for your patience, daily love, and encouragement, and for being the best cheerleader I could ever have. I love you, baby! Thank you to my mother for being by my side through the hardest times in my life, for loving me unconditionally, and never giving up on me. Thank you to Emma's doctors, nurses, respiratory therapists, specialists, and occupational therapists, you all helped save my most precious miracle. Thank you, you who are reading this book, your support means everything. I hope my story has inspired you in some way.

About the author

Being a creator and lover of all thing's beauty, Faby Ryan is a creative entrepreneur and writer. She is a proud mother and bilingual advocate and educator of all things preemie-hood and widowhood. Born to Mexican parents and raised in Los Angeles, California, Faby Ryan is a first generation Mexican-American.

Her passion for writing began early on at the young age of nine after discovering the writings of poet Pablo Neruda, which inspired her and awakened a deeper love for writing poetry, short stories, and sharing her words with the world. This gained her a few scholastic writing awards as well as a presidential award and pin.

In 2012, after suffering three miscarriages, the loss of one of her twins, and giving birth to her 1 lb 2 oz micro-preemie surviving twin, Emma, Faby Ryan's mission to tell her story of loss and survival ignited her advocacy toward parents of preemies. She has served as a volunteer for numerous platforms such as the Ronald McDonald House Charities and women's shelters, and she has also participated and raised money toward March of Dimes/March for Babies every year since. Together with her daughter, Emma, she started her Give-Joy Project as a way to give back for her miracle; a project to support and let other parents of preemies currently in Neonatal Intensive Care Units know they are not alone.

In 2015, after losing her husband, Faby Ryan began a second mission in sharing her grief journey as a young widow and solo parent. She started an online private support group called *Widowed Solo Mommy* which she plans to turn into a podcast. Her story has been published multiple times in online media platforms such as *Love What Matters,* a publication which features real life stories. Faby has made it her life's mission to tell her story of survival hoping it might help others going through life's hardships.

Faby currently lives in Lakewood, California with her daughter, Emma, and her fur baby, Belle. When she is not writing, sharing, or advocating, you can find Faby doing one of the things she loves most: spending time with family and friends or adventuring the great outdoors with Emma, hiking, exploring, traveling, and #ShowingEmmytheWorld.

This book is for anyone who has ever experienced the downsides of life. The dark times. The hardship. The struggles. And for who, at one point or another, has felt alone. Please know you are not alone. This book is meant to help inspire you to live a full, beautiful life and find joy in spite of the hardship life has thrown at you.

http://www.fabyryan.com
Instagram @iam.fabyryan
If you find yourself in need of support from a community who can understand you, look her up on Facebook @widowedsolomommy

Until we meet again...